Art Detective

Art Detective

How to Research Your Paintings, Antiques & Collectables

MADELEINE MARSH

PELHAM BOOKS

For Jessamy, who commissioned this book,
for Joshua, conceived at the same time,
and for Jon with love

PELHAM BOOKS

Published by the Penguin Group
27 Wrights Lane, London w8 5tz
Viking Penguin Inc., 375 Hudson Street, New York, New York 10014, USA
Penguin Books Australia Ltd, Ringwood, Victoria, Australia
Penguin Books Canada Ltd, 10 Alcorn Avenue, Toronto, Ontario, Canada m4v 3b2
Penguin Books (NZ) Ltd, 182–190 Wairau Road, Auckland 10, New Zealand

Penguin Books Ltd, Registered Offices: Harmondsworth, Middlesex, England

First published March 1993
Copyright © Madeleine Marsh 1993

Typeset by Datix International Limited, Bungay, Suffolk
Typeset in Monophoto Bembo 11½/12½ pt
Printed in England by Clays Ltd, St Ives plc

A CIP catalogue record for this book is available from the British Library.

ISBN 0 7207 1993 3

The moral right of the author has been asserted.

Contents

Foreword

As presenter of the *Antiques Roadshow* for the last eleven years, I have seen at first hand the huge wealth of antiques and collectables that exists in private homes throughout Britain, and the enormous interest that they inspire, not only in their owners, but also in the general public who tune in to watch the programme in the millions. As the lengthy and patient queues at every *Roadshow* demonstrate, people have an irrepressible urge to discover more about their possessions, many cherishing the secret hope that they might be valuable, and everybody wanting to resolve their own little mystery.

Now you no longer have to wait for the *Roadshow* to come to town in order to find out about your family heirlooms. *Art Detective* fills a rare and surprising gap in the market that is increasingly flooded with publications. In a direct, practical and entertaining fashion, Madeleine Marsh tells you how to investigate your work of art, consult libraries and museums and find the right expert to answer your questions. Madeleine is a journalist as well as a professional art researcher, and she demystifies, without devaluing, the basic process of art-historical investigation, making it accessible to everyone and, above all, enjoyable.

No matter how many *Roadshows* I and my colleagues take part in, I never cease to be amazed at the apparently endless supply of objects in homes across the country, just waiting to be discovered. With the expert assistance of *Art Detective*, perhaps they will be.

Acknowledgements

I would like to thank Roger Houghton for his good-humoured patience in waiting for this book, and Arianne Burnette for her conscientious and sympathetic editing. No mother can work without complete confidence in her childcare and I would also like to thank Sia, Lipe, and Nia, who made me understand why Tonga is referred to as the friendly isles.

This book could not have been conceived without the assistance and co-operation of the museums, dealers, auction houses, libraries and myriad institutions and private individuals who all took time to answer my letters and telephone calls and, in many instances, to see me in person. Though there are simply too many names to mention here, I am profoundly grateful to every source and institution referred to throughout the book.

In particular, I would like to thank Armin B. Allen (ceramics), Charles Avery (sculpture), Sarah Barter Bailey (arms and armour), David Batty (ceramics), Charles Beare (musical instruments), Michael Bell (silver), Roger Bluett (Oriental antiquities), John Bly (furniture), British Antique Dealers' Association, The British Museum (staff throughout the departments), Andrew Burne (glass), Peter Christie (bronzes), Christie's (staff throughout the departments), Frances Collard (furniture), James Collingridge (silver), John Davies (frames), Peter de V. B. Dewar (heraldry), Jeremy Evans (clocks and watches), Deborah Gage (ceramics), Michael C. German (arms and armour), Catherine Harvey (Oriental art and antiquities), Christopher Hawkings (furniture), Jeanette Hayhurst (glass), Jonathan Horne (ceramics), Philip Ward Jackson (sculpture), Tobias Jellynek (furniture), Paul Johnson (silver), Titus Kendall, Rachel Leigh (dolls), Martin Levy (furniture), Clive Loveless (carpets), P. McAskie (toys), Alan Marcuson and the staff of *Hali* magazine (carpets), Tina Miller (clocks and watches), Jeremy Montague (musical instruments), Anthony Mould (paintings), Richard Ormond and all the staff at the National Maritime Museum and those departments concerned with scientific instruments, Christopher Proudfoot (domestic machinery), Raffety (clocks and watches), Miki Slingsby (photography), Sotheby's (staff throughout the departments), Andrew Morley Stephens, Mayorcas (textiles), Charles Truman (silver), the Victoria & Albert Museum (staff throughout the departments), Mary Wise (ceramics).

Additional thanks to Hugh Scully, Lord Lewin of Greenwich, Peter Marsh, Nicky Marsh and my husband, Jonathan Lewin, for his support both emotional and editorial.

Introduction

To research a work of art you must become a detective. Your evidence is in the article itself: the scribbled signature on a painting, the design of a piece of furniture, the mark on a porcelain pot. Armed with notebook, pencil, and sometimes even a magnifying glass, you can then hunt down further clues in libraries and museums across Britain. You will need to question expert witnesses – curators, specialists, and dealers – and follow up their testimony in books and private archives. One fact leads to another, and as you piece your case together, your object turns from a sterile antique into a living story.

At its best, research can tell you not only who painted your picture, but also why it was painted, which works relate to it, how much it originally cost, where it was hung and who commissioned it. Every object has a social as well as an artistic past: whether you are investigating a picture or a table, you are also unravelling a strand of human history, and that is what makes it enjoyable.

In addition to the thrill of the chase, research can also considerably enhance the value of your piece. A Regency desk commands a certain price. If the same piece is proved to be by a known craftsman, this sum increases. If further investigations reveal that the desk was commissioned by George IV and presented to one of his mistresses, the value will be higher still. The more you find out about an object, the more it can be worth and the more interesting it becomes.

It is not the aim of this book to turn the reader into an 'expert'. Only years of handling works can provide the *Antiques Roadshow* type of knowledge that enables a dealer or curator to identify a Chippendale chair or a Richard Dadd painting at a single glance. However, you do not need to be an art specialist to become an art detective.

Museums and libraries are open to all, though, like icebergs, seven-eighths of their resources lie below the surface. Specialists in every field can be consulted easily, once you know how to find and approach them. Until now there has been no comprehensive practical guide to exploiting this wealth of hidden material and expertise that could enable you to trace the story of an object from its corner in your living room to its rightful place in history.

Art Detective will provide you with the information necessary to conduct these investigations: how to start off, where to get free advice, which museums and libraries to use, what the seminal books are, and where to find those authorities who might help you to solve your case.

Institutions are included from every corner of Great Britain, and occasionally beyond, but the largest proportion of the sources mentioned is to be found in London. London is one of the great art capitals of the world, both commercially and academically. Major national museums, leading dealers and specialists, the principal auction houses, and some of the finest libraries in the world exist side by side and can be visited with ease and speed. Sherlock Holmes made London the centre of his operations and for the art detective, too, there is no better base.

While providing a guide for your investigations, *Art Detective* cannot guarantee their ultimate success. Sometimes your researches will be more successful than you could possibly have imagined – you will solve your mystery and uncover a whole treasure trove of fascinating information. Occasionally you might find out more than is actually good for you, when your Gainsborough is revealed to be a copy, or your eighteenth-century pot a twentieth-century fake – the art

detective should always keep an eye out for the art criminal
or faker. However, it is possible that you will discover little
or nothing at all. Even the greatest detectives have their
unsolved crimes and you might never find out who painted
that charming little watercolour, or the story behind granny's
favourite chair. 'The more featureless and commonplace a
crime is,' complained Sherlock Holmes, 'the more difficult it
is to bring it home'; the same is true for the art detective.

Nevertheless, even when you fail to find any specific
information about your object, you can still learn about its
general history: the contemporary fashions that shaped your
chair or that influenced the style of your painting. At the end
of your researches you still might not know who produced
your work or to whom it belonged, but you will certainly
understand it better, and will be able to appreciate it more.

How to use this book

Part One sets out a general procedure of investigation that
can be applied to any object or work of art, whatever its
nature. It also contains background information relevant to
every subject covered. Whether you are investigating a fine
painting or a furry teddy bear, read this section before
moving on to the chapter most useful to you.

In **Part Two** chapters are divided by subject matter for easy
reference. Each one follows a similar format, providing a
guide to examining the object, to investigating it in libraries,
and to finding the best specialist sources to assist with your
enquiries. Each chapter gives a detailed selection of relevant
museums and institutions, and suggests a short list of recommended reference books.

The **Appendix** is a directory of all the museums mentioned,
listing addresses, telephone numbers and opening times.

At the back of the book there is '**The Art Detective's
Notebook**', which consists of a series of blank pages, so that
you can compile your own list of addresses, names and details
essential to your personal investigations.

The reader is advised throughout to treat this publication as a tool. Write on it, take notes and update information where necessary. If you come across any material that you feel should be included in a revised and expanded edition, please send it to me, Madeleine Marsh, care of the publishers.

What Every Art Detective Needs to Know

1
The Detective Prepares the Case

While each chapter contains specific advice about what to look for in different fields, certain general rules and a similar procedure can be applied to any work of art, be it a painting or a piece of pottery.

Whatever the object, the art detective's investigation can be simplified into three main areas:

1. *The physical evidence:* a detailed examination of the object itself.

2. *The creation of the object:* the major area of investigation – who made it, where and when it was produced, how it relates to the career of its maker and works of the period – in brief, a complete decorative history.

3. *The provenance:* a term used to describe the progress of a work of art from the artist's studio to your living room. For example, who are the different people who have owned it over the years? Was it ever exhibited or sold at auction? This information forms a social and commercial history.

Where should you begin? 'It is a capital mistake to theorise before one has data,' noted Sherlock Holmes, and like any investigator, the art detective should first gather together all extant clues.

I. Examine the Object

Your most important piece of evidence is the object itself, so begin by examining it closely. Look over it, underneath it, inside it and behind it, and try to compile the following checklist:

1. *Title of object:* Write down, very simply, what the object is: i.e. a portrait of two ladies in white dresses seated in a garden, a set of six dining room chairs, a ceramic plate decorated with flowers.

2. *Artist, maker, factory:* Do you have a name to go with your work? Transcribe or photograph any signatures, marks or labels, noting down anything you find written or marked on any part of the piece, including numbers, dots and miscellaneous squiggly bits.

3. *Medium:* What is the object made from or painted on? Do not worry if you cannot identify the material precisely and just write down a generalisation: wood, pottery, glass, oil on canvas, watercolour, etc.

4. *Measurements:* Measure the object in both inches and centimetres.

5. *Description:* Jot down a brief description of the piece, highlighting any particularly interesting features of design or decoration.

II. Collect Circumstantial Evidence

Having extracted as much information as you can from the object itself, it is time to look for circumstantial evidence.

If the object is inherited, write down any family traditions or stories associated with it. Collect together any relevant bills, letters or papers. Make a list of the family members to whom the object has belonged, complete with, if it is not too difficult, their dates of birth and death, which will help to set the object in some sort of context. Be cautious, however, about affixing a date to your piece from this evidence.

According to almost every dealer that I have talked to in the preparation of this book, one of the most common mistakes people make with their cherished possessions is to assume that they are old. Just because Great Aunt Flo (1900–1976) left a teapot to your mother, who gave it to you, this does not automatically make it three generations old – perhaps she bought it new in 1960.

If you purchased the object from a shop or at auction, try to discover who originally owned it, what part of the country it came from and if it belonged to a house of any importance. There is a likelihood that if the dealer has not already disclosed this information at the time of sale, he either won't know or won't tell you, since discretion is paramount in the art world, but it is always worth trying.

This is the first stage of your 'provenance' investigation, and possibly the last stage as well, since you might not come across any further information. Nevertheless, even if your only record is the receipt from your local antique shop, make sure you preserve it. It is always a good idea to keep a record of where and when you bought something and how much it cost. Not only are you creating your own provenance for any future art detectives, but it is also useful for insurance purposes.

III. PHOTOGRAPH THE OBJECT

As you travel round the libraries of Britain, you are unlikely to want to take your work of art with you. A photograph is an essential tool, both for your own researches and to show to the relevant specialist or museum, particularly if your item is too large, too fragile or too valuable to transport. A good photograph is also vital in case a real detective should ever have cause to investigate the disappearance of your wonderfully researched object. Although a simple snapshot will do, it must be as clear as possible. All a fuzzy photo will tell an expert is that you are a bad photographer. You do not want to make your painting look like an Impressionist if it isn't one already.

It is worth spending some time taking a reasonable picture,

and professional fine art photographer Miki Slingsby offers the following advice. First, use colour film and a focusing camera. If you do not have the right kind of camera, see if you can borrow one. Use a tripod, or at least balance the camera on something solid.

Try not to mix natural and artificial light, since this can alter the colour of the object. Where possible, use daylight and photograph it either outside or in a room with large windows. Avoid bright sunshine; the best light of all is that provided by a typically British overcast day.

Highlight your antique by using a plain but contrasting background: i.e. photograph a piece of white china against a black cloth, or a bronze against a piece of white paper. For large objects, such as furniture, use something like a sheet. If you are photographing a mirror or a glass-fronted cabinet and want to minimise reflections, cover the surface with hairspray. For glass, stick some greaseproof paper up against a window, and photograph the glass object against it. This provides a lovely opalescent light.

When photographing paintings, remove the glass if possible. If this is too difficult or you risk damaging the work, you will need to control the lighting, so photograph the object indoors. The same applies to paintings that are very highly varnished.

While it is difficult to prevent glass from reflecting without obscuring the image, you can make sure that the only reflection is black. Photograph the painting in a darkened room where the picture is the only thing lit. If you are using a flash, you should avoid light bouncing off the centre of the picture. Use an extension lead so that while you are standing in front of the painting, the flash is off to one side. If possible, use two flash lights, placed obliquely, one on either side of the picture so that it is evenly lit. If you have only one, place a piece of white card on the other side so that it will reflect the light. If you cannot distance your flash from your camera, take the photograph from an angle. The human brain can understand that a picture is off-key but the human eye, however perspicacious, cannot see through reflections.

If you are not using a flash, place two anglepoise lamps, again at an oblique angle, on either side of the painting. Use

Tungsten film, a slide film that is specially adapted for artificial light, and again make sure that the surroundings are dark so that you and your camera do not star as the central figures in your picture.

Whatever you are photographing, set up your picture carefully. If the object has different decorations on the front and the back, then photograph each side, and take individual shots of any particularly important features of design or decoration. Both with overall shots and close-ups of details, be very aware of what is happening through the lens; check the depth of field, light and shade, and focus. Above all, don't wobble. The most important thing about your picture is that it should be sharp.

You should now have a written description of your object, an account of its known provenance, and – with luck – a clear photograph. It is time to begin your investigation.

2
The Investigation

Having prepared your case and collected all the available data, there are now two courses you can follow: you can embark on your own research or you can seek specialist advice. The best solution is a combination of the two.

If you have some evidence to go on – the signature on a painting, a mark on a pot – then it is worth doing some preliminary detective work and you will need to find a library where you can look up your item. The more you discover for yourself, the easier it is to select the best expert or institution to give you further help. If you find in an art dictionary that the J. Painter who signed your picture is in fact Sir Joshua Painter R.A., eighteenth-century British portraitist, you can then go to the National Portrait Gallery, to the Royal Academy Library and perhaps to the respected Bond Street dealer who specialises in Sir Joshua's works. Books can not tell you if your work of art is a fine example or a fake, but they can help pinpoint the right person to do so.

I. LIBRARIES: GENERAL ADVICE

Specialist libraries and reference books are included in the individual chapters, but, whatever your subsequent needs, your first step should be to phone your local reference library to find out where your nearest art history library is, or at least which branch stocks the most art books. There you will find the dictionaries and basic reference works to help you begin your investigations.

Once you have gathered together clues from books and expert witnesses, your subsequent enquiries can take you to any number of different libraries and record offices, and could include looking at a wide range of both published and unpublished material. Chapters 3 and 4 outline the process of library and archive investigation in greater detail and provide a practical guide to some of the most useful institutions.

No matter which library you are going to visit, it might be helpful to follow a few basic rules. Always check the opening times, because libraries are notoriously idiosyncratic and seem to have an uncanny knack of closing for stocktaking the one week in the year you need to use them. Some smaller libraries shut for lunch, and even with those that don't, the service between 12 and 2 often slows down.

Certain libraries require a letter of recommendation either to obtain a reader's ticket or to consult restricted-access material. The letter should be from someone who sounds respectable – an employer, your supervisor, or a professional friend – and should explain that you need to use academic facilities in the course of serious historical research. It might be a good idea to keep two or three copies of this letter.

The larger the library you are using, the more likely it is that its material will not be on open shelves, but in library stockrooms. This means that you will have to fill out a slip to order up each book you want to look at. Depending on where individual libraries store their books, this can take anything from ten minutes to an hour to twenty-four hours if books are stored off the premises. When using an unfamiliar library, it is worth telephoning in advance just to check how long you should expect to wait, and though it might seem like taking coals to Newcastle, bring along something to read.

Useful things to carry with you include a pencil, since when consulting rare books or manuscripts you are often not allowed to use ink or a biro, and ten pence pieces for the photocopier. As a general rule of thumb, and if possible, it is nearly always better to photocopy than to transcribe information yourself, particularly if it is of any great length. This will not only save time, but also ensures accuracy, as it is irritatingly easy to misspell an unfamiliar name or to transpose a digit in an all-important date.

Another useful tip is always to write down the author, title, publication date and press-mark (the library reference number) of the books from which you have extracted your information. Although this might seem boring, it is important on several counts. First, it provides a source to prove that your research is not simply the result of an overactive imagination. Secondly, if you keep a record of the books you have consulted, you will not forget and re-order the same volumes by mistake, and lastly, should you need to see them again you already have the press-mark, so you will not have to waste time going through the library catalogue, and you might even be able to order the books by phone.

Never be afraid to ask the librarian's advice. People who work in libraries are, in my experience, generally helpful and frequently specialists in the library's particular field. A simple question can save an hour's futile wandering about.

II. FINDING THE EXPERT WITNESSES

If you have no idea what your object is and no evidence to go on, then you will need a specialist to point you in the right direction. Perhaps you want a valuation; possibly you have gathered as much information as you can from libraries, and you now require expert help. Fortunately, there are a number of options and, better still, most of them are free.

AUCTION HOUSES
For a free basic identification and valuation, take your item to the front desk of one of the major auction houses. Although

their head offices tend to be in London, there are regional branches across Britain where, if they cannot answer your questions directly, they will know someone who can.

When valuing your object, the auctioneer will give you a brief assessment and an estimate of the price that he would expect it to fetch at auction. Remember that this is a different and generally inferior figure to both the insurance value and the sum that a Bond Street dealer might charge. So if your porcelain pot, insured for £1,500, is only estimated at £750, do not be upset by the auctioneer. Also be wary of expecting your work of art to fetch a specific sum just because an apparently similar piece recently broke all auction records.

For example, ever since 1989, when Sotheby's sold a Steiff bear for an astonishing £50,000, the auction houses have been inundated with cuddly toys in various stages of dribbled-over decrepitude. Few of them are worth £50, let alone £50,000, which was a freak and probably unique price reached solely because on one specific day two people happened to want the same item desperately. The final figure had little to do with the bear, and everything to do with the bidders.

The antique price guides published annually by firms such as Millers are useful sources of reference, both for their photographs and their list of current market values. However, many of these entries are provided by dealers, who will often include their best pieces and prices, and there is rarely any information about the circumstances of the sale or the condition of the object. As James Collingridge, deputy chairman of Christie's, advises, these books are guides and not gospels: do not automatically expect your work to fetch the same sum, and use any price guide with circumspection.

Do not be frightened to take your treasures to the auction houses. The people there are happy to see anything in the hope of striking pay-dirt. They are also used to dealing with a whole range of objects and customers. 'There are more antiques per square mile in Britain than anywhere in Europe,' notes David Batty proudly, and as ceramics adviser to both Sotheby's and the *Antiques Roadshow*, he should know.

The auction houses provide an extremely comprehensive service. In addition to valuing and, they hope, selling your work of art, they can arrange everything from insurance to shipping, while their financial experts will advise you on capital gains, transfer tax and sales to the nation. For research purposes, they offer an accessible free information service, and a good jumping-off point. Make use of it.

Main Offices of the Principal London Auction Houses

Bonhams
Montpelier Galleries
Montpelier Street
London SW7 1HH
Tel: 071 584 9161

Christie's
8 King Street
London SW1Y 6QT
Tel: 071 839 9060

Phillips
101 New Bond Street
London W1Y 9LG
Tel: 071 629 6602

Sotheby's
34 New Bond Street
London W1A 2AA
Tel: 071 493 8080

DEALERS
Dealers can provide a wonderful source of knowledge both for helping you with initial identifications and for more in-depth research. Many are recognised as being among the leading academic experts in their field. 'If it's your *own* money you are spending, it concentrates the brain wonderfully,' one respected furniture dealer told me glumly. 'An art-historical mistake can spell financial disaster.' Dealers are used to looking at a wide range of objects and are necessarily *au fait* with current market prices. Some are happy to look at objects out of interest; others will give you an assessment and valuation for an agreed fee.

Remember that dealers do not provide a public service, and if you want to consult them purely for information, you will need to chat them up a little. Either make an appointment or pick a time when their shop is unlikely to be busy, be charming and polite, and do not begin by saying, 'I don't want to buy anything', since this might only encourage them to switch off. Remember that from their point of view, you could be, as perhaps you are, an embryo collector with whom they could build up a long and profitable relationship.

Finally, as a general rule, if a dealer, or indeed anybody

else, should offer to buy your work of art, it is only sensible to get one or two independent valuations.

> The most important thing to remember when taking your object to show an expert is to pack it properly. 'Don't use tea towels,' begs David Batty, who recommends newspaper or, better still, bobbly plastic for fragile items. Also, do not attempt to overclean or restore your object. Most experts would rather see the natural patina of age than the cleansing power of Vim, and antique restoration is *always* best left to the professionals.
>
> If your item is too large or too fragile to transport, take along your photographs and details. Do not forget to have the measurements with you, otherwise an expert might find himself looking at a picture of what is clearly a lovely eighteenth-century table, with absolutely no means of knowing if it was made for a dolls' house or a country mansion. 'Indeed, if you can tell what size a piece of furniture is simply from a photograph, then it won't be eighteenth century!' claims Batty's *Roadshow* colleague, furniture dealer John Bly.

How to Find the Right Dealer

Obviously you have nothing to lose by consulting your local antique shop. Good antiques fairs can bring a range of potentially helpful experts together under one roof. At some of the major fairs there will be a desk to which you can take objects for identification.

The way to get the best information is to find an established dealer, with an academic and not simply a commercial passion for his subject, who specialises in your area of interest. There are two main bodies you can contact: the British Antique Dealers' Association (BADA) and the London and Provincial Antique Dealers' Association (LAPADA). BADA is the trade association for Britain's top 500 antique dealers and the staff at their London headquarters will be able to recommend the nearest and/or best person for you to consult. They publish a list of members which indexes dealers by location, name and speciality, and they also provide information about

restorers, antiques fairs, packers, etc. BADA offers its own
Antique Assessment Service to the public, in which a panel
of not less than three experts will provide a written opinion of
an object, including date, description and authentication for
a fee of £172.50 at the time of writing. LAPADA has
a wider, somewhat less exclusive membership, and offers a
computerised information service. In my experience, both of
these societies provide extremely efficient services and offer
useful shortcuts to finding the right expert.

British Antique Dealers' Association (BADA)
20 Rutland Gate
London SW7 1BD
Tel: 071 589 4128

London and Provincial Antique Dealers' Association
(LAPADA)
535 King's Road
London SW10 0SZ
Tel: 071 823 3511

Another address that might be helpful is:

The Society of London Art Dealers
91 Jermyn Street
London SW1Y 6JB
Tel: 071 930 6137

Other sources for finding good dealers include specialist collectors' magazines, specific trade societies, such as the Antique
Doll Dealers' Association of Great Britain, and, best of all,
word of mouth.

MUSEUMS
Britain's museums are a treasure trove for the art detective.
They offer instant and free access to expert opinion, and
many possess helpful study collections and archives that are
open to the public by arrangement. However, they must be
used properly.

   Although a museum is an obvious place to go if you know
nothing about your object, in other circumstances it should
be the last port of call rather than the first. Look up as much

as you can in your local reference library before visiting a museum. The more specific your enquiry and the more you can tell the museum staff, the more they will be able to tell you.

You are using the museum for specialist advice. If you go to the curator saying, 'I want to know all about eighteenth-century art', all you are likely to receive is a strained smile and directions to the local library. If, however, you visit with a specific question about a single piece of work, or a defined area, the expert help and knowledge of the staff can be invaluable.

Identifications

Most museums will give opinions or attributions on objects brought in by the public. Some have particular consultation times when they will look at works, while you must make a specific appointment with others. Whatever the system, always telephone the museum beforehand so that you can arrange to see the most appropriate person. There is no point turning up with a piece of Sèvres only to discover that the French porcelain expert is away having a baby.

If you cannot take the item along in person, write a letter; again, find out which department or member of staff can best answer your enquiries before you write. Enclose a good photograph and as much information about the article as possible, including marks, measurements, and any other details that might be appropriate. Keep the information clear and concise; do not write essays on the subject which will take time to read. Be patient if it takes a while to receive an answer, and wait three to four weeks before contacting the museum again. A self-addressed stamped envelope is a good idea, since a first-class stamp is often more likely to inspire a swift reply than the most impassioned pleading.

Whatever means you choose, make sure that your initial approach is courteous and demonstrates your genuine academic interest in the museum's help and facilities. Afterwards, if someone has given you their time and assistance, a thank-you letter is a good idea, especially if at some stage you need to come back with further enquiries. (The same applies to any other 'expert witness' who has helped you.)

Remember that while museums will give academic help and, in some cases, can provide advice on restoration, *they do not give valuations*. That is the province of the auction houses and the dealers.

Museum Libraries and Archives

Some museums, such as the Victoria & Albert, have official fine art libraries that the public can visit. Many museums also have departmental libraries and archives that can be opened to the 'serious researcher' upon request. Often these contain the most wonderful material: picture libraries collated by generations of hard-working curators; in-depth studies on everything from finger rings to chimneypieces; rare inventories and manuscripts. Departmental libraries are working tools for museum staff and are only available to the public in a semi-official way. If you need to use their material, you must make an appointment. Establish beforehand which areas you want to look at, since you will not be able to browse. Don't waste either your or the curator's time by using the museum to consult books you could find in your local reference library.

When visiting the departmental libraries, you will often have to be signed in and out by a member of staff, so don't decide that you want to go out for a cup of coffee five minutes after your arrival. It is likely, since you are handling museum material, that you will be supervised. Be prepared to fit in with staff requirements. Often there is no one available to supervise at lunchtime, so that is when you should go and battle with the schoolchildren and the tourists in the museum café.

Don't be a pain in the neck, but equally don't be afraid to ask questions, since the curator could be invaluable in pointing you in the right direction. In my experience, museum staff tend to be extremely helpful and only too happy to discuss their area of expertise. Even if they cannot answer your question directly, they are often able to put you in touch with other experts and to provide clues and suggestions which you can follow up later.

Choosing Your Museum

Each chapter in Part Two suggests museums and specialist collections that might be able to assist you with your enquiries. In many cases, I have included information about museum libraries and archives available to the public, and the identification or opinion services on offer. The Museum Directory in the Appendix gives a complete list of all the museums mentioned, with addresses, telephone numbers and opening times.

The field is far too wide, and my space too limited, to include more than an abbreviated selection of museums. At the local library, however, you should be able to find a number of current museum directories, cataloguing museums and galleries in Britain and abroad. These tend to be indexed geographically, but some also include a subject index, so that you can find a museum specialising in your field. Your local museum is always worth consulting for information.

Bibliography

The Directory of Museums and Living Displays, London, Macmillan, 1981

The International Directory of Arts, Germany, Art Address Verlag Muller (consult the most recent edition)

Museums and Galleries in Great Britain and Ireland – annual publication by British Leisure Publications

The Museums Year Book – annual publication by the Museums Association

Chapel, Jeannie and Gere, Charlotte. *The Fine and Decorative Art Collections of Britain and Ireland*, London, Weidenfeld & Nicolson, 1985

Hudson, Kenneth and Nicholls, Ann. *The Cambridge Guide to the Museums of Britain and Ireland*, Cambridge, Cambridge University Press, 1987

SPECIALIST SOCIETIES

There are innumerable specialist societies in Britain concentrating on every conceivable theme from fine artists to Dinky Toys. They can be a useful source of advice and are a good place to encounter leading experts and enthusiasts in a particular field.

A short selection of these societies appears in the following chapters. Since, in many instances, their contact addresses are personal and change with the appointment of a new secretary, I have concentrated on organisations with a permanent address or linked with a museum or other public institution. For further information and current details, contact a museum specialising in the same general area as the society itself. *Antique Collecting: The Journal of the Antique Collectors' Club* (5 Church Street, Woodbridge, Suffolk IP12 1DS, Tel: 0394 385501) includes a list of regional antique societies and clubs; addresses can also be obtained from dealers and specialist magazines.

MISCELLANEOUS WITNESSES

Apart from the more usual centres of artistic and academic reference, your investigations could eventually lead you in any number of different directions. If your object commemorates a particular sporting event, the relevant sporting association might be able to help. Should it relate to a specific sect or society, contact their representative body for advice (also see chapter 23). If the company that produced your work is still in operation, get in touch with their head office. Many firms will have an archivist, or, failing that, at least some faithful retainer with a knowledge of the firm's history and products. Similarly, there might be a guild, trade association or worshipful company who might be able to help.

In the past, my own work has taken me to the Jockey Club to research the details of horses in nineteenth-century racing pictures, to Jermyn Street tobacconists for advice on snuff and snuffboxes, and to the Hoover factory for information on antique domestic appliances. It is not only the art historian who can help the art detective. On one occasion I was working for Sotheby's on a collection of jewellery given by Edward VII to Mrs Keppel, his final and favourite mistress. One of the gifts was a small nautical brooch, consisting of four enamelled signalling flags. It appeared little more than a pretty and innocent love token, until a communications officer from the Royal Navy decoded its scurrilous message: 'Position quarterly and open. I am about to fire a Whitehead torpedo ahead'.

As these examples demonstrate, it is impossible to predict what sources you might eventually need. While *Art Detective* cannot guide you in particular cases, your object can. Look at the work, use your common sense and allow it to point you in the right direction.

Be flexible and imaginative in your choice of 'expert witnesses' and never be afraid of contacting an unfamiliar organisation. Do, however, be as charming as possible, since it is likely they will have no formal system for dealing with such enquiries and you will have to rely on the goodwill of often hard-pressed staff.

Finally, should you require the services of a professional art detective, contact Provenance Ltd. Tel: 081 741 0410. Fax: 081 741 4947.

3

Books and Libraries: Conducting Further Enquiries

I. PUBLISHED MATERIAL

As an art detective your ultimate goal is to compile a complete case history of the object in question, with information on the piece itself, the person who made it and the people who owned it. As you proceed with your enquiries, you will gradually build up a bibliography of relevant publications.

Whatever the nature of your object, the first books you will need to consult are dictionaries and general works of reference. In each chapter and for every major subject, I have included a selection of the best books to begin with – the basic bibles recommended by academics, dealers and other experts.

These works, many of which are kept on open display in libraries, will give you your first pieces of hard evidence – dates of an artist, details of a porcelain factory, a description of a teddy bear – and they will also provide you with other major clues by listing relevant museums, specialist archives, and, above all, other sources of published information.

Apart from books devoted to the fine and decorative arts, reference sources could include literally anything from privately printed memoirs to national encyclopaedias. Your final bibliography could refer you to articles in magazines or newspapers, to sale and exhibition catalogues, to single pages in the most obscure volumes or, if your artist or craftsman is sufficiently famous, to an individual monograph or biography.

> For the applied arts as a whole, a marvellous first reference book is John Fleming and Hugh Honour's *Dictionary of the Decorative Arts* (London, Viking, 1989), which provides useful information on many different subjects.

MAGAZINES AND PERIODICALS

You might have discovered from a reference book or catalogue that works by your artist appeared in an *Art Journal* review of an exhibition in 1882, in a feature on the man himself in *The Burlington Magazine* dated February 1945, and in an article on local painters past and present in a recent provincial journal. By checking these sources you might not only discover more about the artist, but you could also find some interesting comments on his work – a good period quote never goes amiss – and, in the best of all possible worlds, you might come across a reference to or even an illustration of your own object. The latter is not a likely enough possibility to be worth holding your breath for, but it can and does happen.

If you know that your painting or object came from a country house of some importance, then try turning to *Country Life*, which has published an index of all the major houses and buildings covered by its articles from 1900 to 1984. Since these often include photographs of interiors and information about art collections and patrons, the magazine can prove a useful source of reference both for provenance material and pictorial evidence. I once researched a splendid pair of eighteenth-century andirons (firedogs) which wealthy American clients had purchased from the contents sale of an English country mansion. In a *Country Life* issue from the early 1900s, I found an illustrated article on the house, and there in the centre of a photograph of the baronial hall were my andirons, surrounded by stuffed animals and portraits of all the people who had owned them in the past: a lovely period picture and a graphic illustration of their provenance.

There are many art and antiques magazines, and in my experience some of the more useful periodicals include:

The Antique Collector (est 1931)
Apollo (est 1925)
The Art Journal (1839–1911)
The Builder (est 1843)
The Burlington Magazine (est 1903)
Connoisseur (est 1901)
Country Life (est 1897)
The Magazine of Art (1878–1904)
The Studio (1893–1960s)

When consulting magazines, or indeed any other publication, make as much use of indexes as possible. Certain journals, such as *The Burlington Magazine*, have published an index to all their articles over the years, which allows you to check quickly for references to your subject.

SALE CATALOGUES
Sale catalogues are another major hunting ground for the art detective. Suppose that your painting or object was sold by Christie's on 12 June 1904. If you trace the catalogue entry, it could tell you not only who sold the item, but also, if the catalogue has been annotated, who bought it and for how much. The National Art Library at the V&A has a major collection of old auction catalogues and Christie's has its own muniments room in St James's (open to the public by appointment, and staffed at present by a charming curator), containing all the company's catalogues from the eighteenth century to the present day.

An invaluable reference book for sales catalogues is Frits Lugt's *Repertoire des Catalogues de Ventes Publiques 1600–1925*, 4 vols, La Haye, Nijhoff, 1938–87. International in scope, the publication covers auctions for which catalogues have been preserved in major libraries around the world. Auctions are catalogued by date and indexed by vendor. Take, for example, a picture or an object said to have belonged to Lord Y in the nineteenth century. Look up Lord Y in the index and you might discover that his collection was sold by

Sotheby's on 10 June 1890, and the catalogue is held at the V&A. You can then consult the volume to see if your work is included.

EXHIBITION CATALOGUES

If you suspect or have proof that your work was exhibited, you should check for an accompanying exhibition catalogue. If the gallery that held the exhibition is still extant, contact them for further information; if it no longer exists, the V&A National Art Library, the Tate Gallery Library and the British Library all house major collections of catalogues. Local museums can be a useful source for provincial exhibitions. Having found your catalogue, be sure to note down all relevant information, including dates, location, the exhibition number of the painting or work of art, and any other details. If it was a major exhibition, it might be worth having a quick look through contemporary periodicals to see if the show or your item has been reviewed or commented upon.

BIOGRAPHICAL INFORMATION

Much of your investigation will consist of tracking down dates and biographical data, not only for the artist or craftsman, but also for the sitter, if you are investigating a portrait, or the previous owners.

The standard general reference book in this field is *The Dictionary of National Biography*, although, as its title suggests, it only deals with figures of some national importance. Many countries have produced similar publications that are available in major libraries, if you are researching a foreign figure. Other useful tomes include *Who's Who* and *Who Was Who*, the chronicle of dead famous people, and publications such as *Burke's Peerage*, which are essential for collecting basic data about Lord Y and his ubiquitous relations (see chapter 7 on heraldry).

The Times, Britain's oldest surviving national daily newspaper and the only one covered by a comprehensive index, is available at most major reference libraries. Its obituaries can be helpful for biographical details, and you might well come across other interesting facts in the main body of the paper. Another good, and indexed, source for obituaries and informative gossip about eighteenth- and nineteenth-century figures is *The Gentleman's Magazine.*

If your subject is of sufficient interest, he might have had a biography devoted to him, or he could appear in other people's memoirs or historical accounts. As you spend time researching a particular period, you get to know who the great gossips and natterers of the age were, whose published reminiscences will contain the juiciest stories – artistic or social – about their contemporaries, and which biographers are the most informative.

Use lateral thinking and allow one book to lead you to another. Say you are researching the story of Miss X, the voluptuous subject of a turn of the century portrait. In the diaries of an Edwardian courtier, you find a single reference to her, when the writer records meeting the said lady at the Derby in the company of her great friend, Lord Y. You then look up the biography of Lord Y, and there in a footnote is a short history of Miss X, along with references to another publication. Compiling biographical information is like putting together an ancient and complicated jigsaw puzzle: sometimes the whole picture will fall into place perfectly, while on other occasions key pieces will be missing and, try as you might, you will never retrieve them.

SIGNS AND SYMBOLS: INTERPRETING ICONOGRAPHY
Depending on what your picture or object is, you might well have to interpret its significance.

What might look like a painting of two dirty old men spying on a naked girl could, in fact, be the religious subject Susanna and the Elders, a story of two dirty old men spying on a naked girl, an Old Testament tale popular with artists from the Renaissance onwards, precisely because it sanctioned the portrayal of female nudity.

Recognising a story, be it sacred or secular, is only part of understanding the artistic and historical iconography of the period. Why does one little girl in your eighteenth-century portrait hold a cherry, while the other wears a coral necklace?

Who are these classical figures flanking your ormolu clock, and why are owls inlaid in the wooden panels of your library desk?

The answers to such questions can often be found in James Hall's *Dictionary of Subjects and Symbols in Art* (rev ed, London, John Murray, 1979). This is an absolutely essential book for the art detective, as it gives a clear account of the classical myths, religious stories and secular themes that make up the vocabulary of Western painting and that are represented throughout the fine and decorative arts.

Ebenezer Cobham Brewer's *Dictionary of Phrase and Fable* (14th rev ed, London, Cassell, 1990) is helpful for looking up symbols and significances. A good dictionary of saints can also be a useful tool, as can a guide to classical figures and heroes.

II. FINDING THE RIGHT LIBRARY

During your investigations you could have recourse to an astounding variety of publications: histories of costume to date a dress; topographical works and pictorial magazines to locate a painted landscape; the catalogues of a toy firm or department store to identify a Dinky car. Whatever your various needs, your first requirement is a good library. Where possible, try to find one where books are kept on open shelves: you can quite easily spend many tedious hours and even days waiting for requested volumes to emerge from the vast depths of a library storeroom and, whether you are a professional or an amateur researcher, you do not want to waste your time. Also, the freedom to browse can often yield much useful information.

NATIONAL COPYRIGHT LIBRARIES

By law, these libraries must receive a copy of every British publication and they also have rich collections of foreign material. You will usually need a letter of recommendation to obtain a user's card. There are five national copyright libraries in Britain and Ireland:

The British Library, London (see below for details)

National Library of Scotland
George IV Bridge
Edinburgh EH1 1EW
Tel: 031 226 4531

National Library of Wales
Aberystwyth
Dyfed SY23 3BU
Tel: 0970 623 816

Cambridge University Library
West Road
Cambridge CB3 9DR
Tel: 0223 333013

The Bodleian Library
University of Oxford
Broad Street
Oxford OX1 3BG
Tel: 0865 277 000

Trinity College Library
College Street
Dublin 2
Ireland
Tel: 010 353 1 772941

III. THE ART DETECTIVE'S GUIDE TO THE LIBRARIES OF LONDON

The following are, in my experience, the most useful London art libraries. To find the best art library in your area, go to your local reference library for advice.

The British Library
Great Russell Street
London WC1B 3DG
Tel: 071 323 7676
Mon, Fri, Sat: 9–5; Tues, Wed, Thurs: 9–9

At the British Library, you should be able to find most of the printed material that you need, with the exception of certain sale and exhibition catalogues. Its foreign collection is also particularly extensive.

Reference works are on open shelves, otherwise everything must be ordered from the catalogue. Depending on where books are stored, some volumes will take fifty minutes to be delivered and others twenty-four hours,† so the best way to use this library is to go and order all your books for the following day or whenever else is convenient. When filling out your application slips, it is a good idea to double-check the press-mark, since a faulty number will elicit supercilious glances from the staff, and possibly another twenty-four-hour wait for your book. Photocopying services are good but expensive, working out at twenty pence per sheet. The library staff are also real sticklers about copyright laws, particularly in regard to photocopying illustrations, which seem to be covered by regulations so arcane and complex that you need a combined degree in law and patience to understand them. Before using the library, you will need to obtain a pass, which can be issued immediately if you have your letter of recommendation.

As a final note, when you leave the building, the staff check through your bag to see that you have not stolen any books, so it is a good idea not to have anything embarrassing in it: a favourite cuddly toy, your dirty washing . . .

NB: Newspapers and most daily and weekly periodicals are kept in the British Library Newspaper Library, Colindale Avenue, London NW9 5HE, Tel: 071 323 7353, Mon–Sat: 10–5.

The London Library
14 St James's Square
London SW1Y 4LG
Tel: 071 930 7705/6
Mon–Sat: 9.30–5.30; Thurs: 9.30–7.30

The London Library wins the art detective's award for the most useful centre of investigations. It is a private lending and reference library that you can join for £100 a year, or £12 for a monthly pass, which allows you to consult books but not to take them away. If you can afford it, membership on whatever basis your research demands is the best investment

† From 1993, the British Library will have moved to its new location in St Pancras. All books will be stored on site, so there should be no more twenty-four-hour waits.

you will ever make and will save you a fortune in time, emotional wear and tear, and the fares that you would otherwise spend rushing to and from other libraries.

The library has a superb general stock; much of its material is equalled only by the major national libraries. Nearly everything is kept on open shelves: you can borrow most of the books and photocopy from them. For a researcher, the London Library is perhaps the nearest thing to heaven. This may sound like an exaggeration, but if you have spent hours waiting for books to appear from storerooms, and offered everything from bribes to your body in an attempt to get a decent photocopying service, you will appreciate what I mean.

As well as umpteen thousand books, pamphlets and catalogues, the library has a fine collection of old and contemporary periodicals, and stocks a full edition of *The Times*. Particularly useful for the art researcher are the Fine and Decorative Arts Room, the Topography Department and the superb history and biography collections.

The Victoria & Albert Museum (V&A)
National Art Library
Cromwell Road
London SW7 2RL
Tel: 071 938 8500
Tues–Sat: 10–5

The V&A National Art Library houses the world's largest collection of books on art, and the collection includes manuscripts as well as printed material. It is the place to go for books on the fine and decorative arts, art periodicals, and exhibition and auction catalogues. For the latter, there is a useful index which allows you to look up auctions by the name of the vendor as well as by location and date – the Owners' Card Index. The collection is wonderful, and you should be able to find most of the material you might need but, unfortunately, in my experience the museum's system does not match up to the quality of its collection.

Books can take anything from twenty minutes to over an hour to arrive, and I have frequently filled out requests for books that turn out to be mislaid, wrongly numbered, or apparently non-existent. The photocopying system used to be antediluvian and is still slow. Staff, however, are invariably helpful and the end result is worth all the minor irritations.

Also part of the National Art Library is the
Archive of Art & Design
23 Blythe Road
London W14 0QF
Tel: 071 603 1514
Tues–Thurs: 10–1, 2–4.30
Contact the curator before visiting.

The archive holds primary source material for the study of art and design in the twentieth century, including the papers of designers, artists, craftsmen and scholars, the archives of businesses and societies concerned with the arts, and exhibition material.

For more basic fine and decorative art research, the Barbican and Westminster Art Libraries both have a good stock of art books and periodicals. The latter has very experienced art library staff; the former is a lending library, which anyone can join, and is very useful if you have a lot of background material to plough through, and you would rather read the books in the comfort of your own home.

Barbican Library
Barbican Centre
Silk Street
Barbican EC2Y 8DS
Tel: 071 638 4141
Mon, Wed–Fri: 9.30–5.30; Tues: 9.30–7.30; Sat: 9.30–12.30

The Westminster Library
Art and Design Library
St Martin's Street
London WC2H 7HP
Tel: 071 798 2038
Mon–Fri: 10–7; Sat: 10–5

Other libraries that might be of use include:

The Design Museum Library
28 Shad Thames
Butlers Wharf
London SE1 2YD
Tel: 071 403 6933
Tues–Sat: 11.30–6.30

The Design Museum Library contains information on design and related subjects. Its books are stored on open shelves.

English Heritage
Photographic Library
Fortress House
23 Savile Row
London W1X 1AB
Tel: 071 973 3338
Mon–Fri: 9–5.15

English Heritage has gathered together a large photographic archive of its own properties and other buildings. The collection includes photographs of exteriors, interiors, and individual furnishings, so it can be very helpful if you are interested in finding out about a particular house or collection. The library is open to the general public, but ring to make an appointment.

★ Royal Borough of Kensington and Chelsea
Central Library
Phillimore Walk
London W8 7RX
Tel: 071 937 2542

The reference and lending library includes a strong fine arts section.

★ London College of Printing
Library and Learning Resources Centre
Elephant and Castle
London SE1 6SB
Tel: 071 735 8484

This houses a large collection of books and periodicals with a concentration in design and media. It also has an important slide library relating to art and design, and poster and illustration collections.

Royal Institute of British Architects (RIBA)
British Architectural Library
66 Portland Place
London WIN 4AD
Tel: 071 580 5533
Mon: 10–5; Tues–Thurs: 10–8; Fri: 10–7; Sat: 10–1.30

With its collections of manuscripts, books, periodicals, drawings and photographs, the RIBA has one of the finest architectural libraries in the world. Architecture is interpreted in its widest sense to include related fields such as interior design, topography and the applied arts.

Though most of the papers relate to the lives and works of British architects, designers, craftsmen, painters and sculptors also feature in the collection. The library is open to the public, so appointments are not necessary. For the art detective, it can be useful for researching architectural drawings, for tracing the history of the great houses and their collections, and for researching furniture and the applied arts designed by architects or created with specific buildings in mind.

★ St Bride's Printing Library
Bride Lane
Fleet Street
London EC4Y 8EE
Tel: 071 353 4660

The St Bride's Printing Library specialises in the history of printing – not of prints! – publishing and related subjects.

★ Swiss Cottage Library
88 Avenue Road
London NW3 3HA
Tel: 071 586 5989

This library houses a general fine arts collection.

★ The Warburg Institute
Woburn Square
London WC1H 0AB
Tel: 071 580 9663

The Warburg Institute focuses on the history of European culture, including art history. Admission is at the discretion of the Director, so a letter of reference is required; make an appointment before you visit. This is definitely a place for the serious scholar rather than the casual investigator.

★ Telephone for opening times.

4
Archives and Local Records: Digging Up The Evidence

I. UNPUBLISHED MATERIAL

In many instances the art detective will have to go beyond books and readily available published material in order to track down the story of an object. This means going to local history libraries and county record offices, digging up contemporary records, deciphering period handwriting, sifting through dusty bundles of yellowing paper tied up with string, and really getting down to the nitty-gritty – and it can be, literally, gritty – of the investigation.

How does the detective set about finding this unpublished material? The books you have consulted might already have pointed you to an archive collection held by a private or public organisation. If you have an address for your artist, or at least some idea of where he or she lived and worked, then you can turn to the relevant local history library for advice and information.

No matter how much or how little evidence you have to go on, one of the best places to begin your investigations is the Royal Commission on Historical Manuscripts, the Mecca of the art detective, or indeed of anybody conducting any form of British historical research.

The Royal Commission on Historical Manuscripts
Quality House
Quality Court
Chancery Lane
London WC2A 1HP
Tel: 071 242 1198
Mon–Fri: 9.30–5

This is an extremely useful source that is open to the public but is surprisingly little known. The Commission provides a guide to the collections of archives and manuscripts held in record offices throughout the country. It does not refer just to art records, so you can use it in several different ways.

Look up your artist or craftsman in the index which, if he or she is included, will refer you to one or several of the many binders that line the walls. These are essentially catalogues of their holdings provided by museums, universities, county record offices, and other organisations. In one volume you might discover that the artist's letters have been preserved at the Royal Academy; in another, that transactions concerning his work for Lord Y may be found in Lord Y's papers at a local library in Leeds; and in a third, that details of his bankruptcy and subsequent sad demise are kept by the Public Record Office.

If you have an unsigned portrait that you know is of Lord Y, and you would like to find out the name of the artist, you can try looking through Lord Y's records to see if there are any references to bills or letters that might help you in your quest.

Similarly, if you have a picture or a piece of furniture or silver that is believed to have come from a famous country mansion, you can look up the name of the house and its owner in the Commission's indexes and then search for any references to household inventories, bills or related papers.

Each index of holdings varies in quality, according to how well individual collections of papers have been catalogued by whoever owns them. If you want to examine the material itself, you will then have to go to the local libraries or institutions mentioned, or you can try writing to them. If there are many sources to go through, you will almost certainly have to visit in person.

II. LOCAL HISTORY LIBRARIES AND COUNTY RECORD OFFICES

The Royal Commission on Historical Manuscripts have compiled a guide, *Record Repositories in Great Britain and Ireland* (published by HMSO), listing the addresses and details of these mines of information. Many county record offices and local history libraries can only be visited by appointment, and it is vital to check the opening times. Some institutions close for lunch; others are only open on certain days; and some seem to shut down every time there is an 'r' in the month. The staff are often passionate enthusiasts about their local area, so do ask their advice. Finally, do not forget your pencil, as ink is invariably forbidden; sometimes a magnifying glass can be useful, particularly if you find yourself dealing with spidery eighteenth-century script.

This is where research becomes a serious business and I can suggest no shortcuts. You could find yourself spending days in a damp and gloomy muniments room going through endless bills and finding accounts for everything from hair powder to gripe water without coming across a single reference to your picture or object.

Nevertheless, there are compensations. There is nothing like bills to give you a sense of the daily life of the people you are researching: you get to know what they ate and drank, where they bought their clothes and what they gave the under-housemaid for Christmas. When I was searching through the household accounts at Windsor Castle for references to a firm of nineteenth-century bronzemakers, I came across all kinds of fascinating trivia that had nothing to do with my quest, such as payments to the royal bed-debugger, who toured the castle on a regular basis to remove the offending creatures from the royal bedrooms.

Letters and personal correspondence can be great fun, particularly if the writer is of a lively or bitchy disposition. There is something enormously exciting about handling a document written in the hand of a famous figure from the past, however trivial it might seem. Again in quest of my bronzemakers, I went through the notebooks and papers of the brilliant and eccentric nineteenth-century Gothic architect

William Burges, for whom they had carried out much work. In the margin of one of his notebooks, next to their itemised account, he had appended a cross note that they were far too expensive, and implied that he certainly wasn't going to use them again. This tiny, throw-away grumble made the characters involved come to life, precisely because it was so mundane.

One of the most enjoyable elements about research is that it reveals craftsman and employer, painter and patron, to be real people and shows that a picture has a story that extends beyond the image depicted on the canvas.

III. LOCAL CLUES AND GENEALOGICAL DETECTION

If you are investigating the history of an individual who lived and worked in a certain area, possibly someone not particularly famous, then the local history library or county record office could well prove to be your major if not your only source of biographical information.

If your subject has not left any specific papers behind, then his or her name will probably not be recorded in the lists at the Royal Commission. Yet they could well appear in material held by the local record office, in post office directories, rate books, parish registers, census forms, requests for planning permission, electoral registers – all those endless, tedious forms that we still fill in today without ever thinking that we are at the same time preserving our names and details for posterity.

Supposing, for example, that on the back of your anonymous nineteenth-century picture, in what appears to be its original frame, you find the following yellowing label:

Edward Everyman
Ormolu Framemaker and Gilder
23 Fitzroy Street
London

Finding out about Mr Everyman might not tell you who

painted your picture, but it could help you date it more precisely. Being only a framer and literally on the periphery of art, Mr Everyman does not appear in any of the standard references works, so where do you look?

The one type of book that is completely undiscriminating in terms of the fame of the people it lists is the post office directory. Directories were produced in the eighteenth century and even earlier, but it was in the nineteenth century that they truly came into their own. Perhaps the most famous is *Kelly's Street Directory*, which from the 1840s onwards listed people by street, name and trade.

Comb through the directories and you might find that Mr Everyman first appears at 23 Fitzroy Street in 1842; he remains there for five years and then moves to 19 Tottenham Court Mews. Thus you have a date for your frame between 1842 and 1847, and possibly a date for your picture as well.

The same process can be applied to any stamp, label or inscription you find on a painting, a piece of furniture or any other object. Perhaps inside your Victorian chest of drawers there is a half-torn label saying only '3 Regent Street'. Look up the street and its number in *Kelly's* over a corresponding period of years to find that between 1853 and 1863 Josiah Bloggs, Fancy Cabinetmaker, lived there.

Directories yield only the most basic information. If you require more biographical details about your subject, you can then take things a stage further by consulting rate books, census returns and local newspapers at the local history library; by tracing birth, death and marriage certificates at St Catherine's House; and by following the standard path of genealogical research. There are many published guides to this most popular form of private detective work and the librarian at your local history library will be able to point you in the right direction.

This form of research is both the most difficult, since you cannot crib from anyone else's expertise, and the most rewarding, since you are really sailing into uncharted waters. It is in the unglamorous surroundings of the local history libraries that the art detective can make his or her greatest discoveries.

GENERAL ADDRESSES

For provincial directories, contact the relevant local history library or county records office. London directories can be consulted at:

Guildhall Library
Aldermanbury
London EC2P 2EJ
Tel: 071 260 1868/1870

Victoria Library
Archives and Local History
160 Buckingham Palace Road
London SW1 9UD
Tel: 071 798 2180
Mon–Fri: 9.30–7; Sat: 9.30–1, 2–5

Registers of births, deaths and marriages since 1837 are held by:

The Office of Population Censuses and Surveys
St Catherine's House
10 Kingsway
London WC2B 6LH
Tel: 071 242 0262.

5

Specialist Bookshops

Fine and decorative art books, particularly if they are old and out of print, can be hideously expensive. If you are only interested in a one-off or very occasional piece of art-detecting, then there is little point investing in works that you might never look at again – you are far better off using the library.

If, however, you have moved on from investigating an individual object to concentrating on a certain field, or if you have decided to collect, or even become an expert witness in your own right, then a selection of relevant reference books is invaluable. Every dealer that I talked to in compiling this book had his or her own library of seminal works both old and new, as well as runs of art periodicals, auction catalogues and innumerable clippings and photographs.

While the art department of any good bookshop will be able to supply you with a reasonable selection of volumes in print, your needs are likely to extend beyond contemporary and readily available publications. Therefore the specialist art bookshops listed below are recommended. Most of them concentrate on out-of-print as well as contemporary works. Their stock is international, covers every aspect of their chosen field, and ranges from the weightiest monograph to the tiniest catalogue. Nobody, with the best will in the world, could describe their wares as cheap, but these shops do offer rare works and a specialist service: you can use their expertise to help compile bibliographies, to identify the best books in your chosen field, and to track down otherwise unobtainable tomes.

Museums often have good bookshops, with books and catalogues – normally in print – relating to the subjects covered by their collections. Dealers in certain fields will also carry related catalogues and monographs, and should be able to recommend a bookshop specialising in their area.

For a possibly cheaper, although much more hit-and-miss alternative, haunt the secondhand bookshops of Britain. Almost invariably there will be an art and antiques section; sometimes you can pick up real bargains and works that are now collectable in their own right. Remainder bookshops can also be good places for a cheap arts purchase, but avoid the endless part-worky type books that have been churned out by the thousand about antiques and artists (the Impressionists are a particular favourite).

Thomas Heneage Art Book Shop
42 Duke Street
St James's
London SW1Y 6DJ
Tel: 071 930 9223

Fine, decorative and applied arts – in and out of print.

Potterton Books
The Old Rectory
Sessay
Thirsk
North Yorkshire Y07 3LZ
Tel: 0845 401218

Fine, decorative and applied arts – in and out of print.

St George's Gallery Books
8 Duke Street
London SW1Y 6BL
Tel: 071 930 0935

Fine, decorative and applied arts – in print.

Sims & Reed
58 Jermyn Street
London SW1Y 6LX
Tel: 071 493 5660

Mostly fine arts – in and out of print.

Zwemmer Art Booksellers
24 Litchfield Street
London WC2H 9NJ
Tel: 071 379 7886

Fine, decorative and applied arts – in and out of print.

Oriental specialists:

John Randall Books
47 Moreton Street
London SW1V 2NY
Tel: 071 630 5331

This shop specialises in Islamic, Indian, Tibetan, South-East Asian and Central Asian Art; the staff can also supply booklists on specialist topics.

Han Shang Tang Ltd
717 Fulham Road
London SW6 5UL
Tel: 071 731 2447

Oriental art and antiquities.

For a list of secondhand and antiquarian booksellers con-centrating on the fine and decorative arts across Great Britain contact:

The Provincial Booksellers' Fairs Association
PO Box 66
Cambridge
CB1 3PD
Tel: 0223 240921.

6
Wrapping Up the Case

I. THE FINAL SOLUTION

It is difficult to predict at the beginning of any investigation how much information you might eventually come up with. You could find virtually nothing, or enough material for an article or even a book. In some cases, you will not be able to get much further than a basic physical description of the object, an approximate date and a country of origin. If the object itself is not of any great interest or value, then this will be sufficient for your needs, and perhaps it was all you wanted in the first place.

Many works, even if they are of the most superlative quality, are destined to remain unsolved mysteries, and try as you might, you will never find out who painted or produced them, to whom they originally belonged, or any of the finer details of their history. In other circumstances, however, you will discover more than you could have thought possible.

A client of mine had a piece of fine French eighteenth-century furniture which had been sold by a Mrs X at Christie's in 1906. While he had enough information about the object, he knew nothing about its former owner, and commissioned me to research her history.

All I had was her name and her London address at the time of the auction. She did not appear in any of the standard biographical dictionaries or accounts of the period, so without much hope I turned to the local history libraries. Within three days, I had uncovered a fascinating story, from rate books, old post office directories, archives and contemporary publications. These revealed Mrs X to be a wealthy and beautiful widow, a prominent figure in London society, and a particularly 'close friend' of Edward VII, a king renowned for his intimacies with beautiful ladies. Although she had been virtually ignored by most of Edward's subsequent biographers, newspapers of the day reported how she acted as his hostess at her Berkeley Square house. The journalists were apparently scandalised when the King granted her a royal residence to live in as her country home, and covered in painstaking detail her ultimate bankruptcy and the sale of all her goods at auction.

This story illustrates how much information can be obtained from the most minimal of clues. Never be put off: you cannot tell what you will find until you begin your investigations. It is also a good example of an appealing provenance. While Mrs X's connections, however illustrious, could not improve the quality of her former furniture, they nevertheless made it more interesting and more valuable. For my client, an American, his work was no longer just an example of French craftsmanship, be it ever so fine, but a little bit of English history and a marvellous conversation piece.

II. WRITING UP THE CASE

Whatever your object is and whatever you find out about it, you will need to organise your information. The following checklist provides a standard format for cataloguing a work of art. It sets out most of the points you might be able to cover, depending on the nature and importance of your object and the ultimate success of your investigations.

1. *Title and description of object.*

2. *Name of artist, maker, factory*: This should be followed by

a short biography of the same (a standard dictionary definition will do).

3. *Signatures, marks or labels*: A full description.

4. *Date*.

5. *Nationality*.

6. *Medium*.

7. *Measurements*.

8. *Provenance*: A list of the previous owners and of sales in which the object has appeared, complete with lot numbers and dates. If the owners are of any interest, as in the case cited above, include their biographical details, complete with any related illustrations, i.e. the photocopy of a portrait, or an article on the house where they and their objects resided.

9. *Exhibitions*: A list of exhibitions in which the object has appeared, with dates and catalogue numbers.

10. *Literature*: A list of books, magazines and other material in which the object has been discussed or illustrated, complete with title, author, date and page number.

11. *Historical research*: A full account of anything and everything you have found out about the history of the object, complete with, where possible, photocopies or illustrations of related works, drawings or any other connected material.

12. *Present-day valuation*.

The checklist is designed to cover every possibility and every type of object. Obviously some categories only apply to works of a certain standing. It is unlikely that granny's favourite table would have appeared in an article or an exhibition, or have belonged to a famous person – so, as with all forms, delete where applicable.

At the end of your investigations, fill in as many points as you can, making your entries as long or as short as seems appropriate. If you do not want to transcribe information yourself, use photocopies, particularly for material such as biographical details that can be taken directly from reference books.

It is impossible to say how long your investigations might take you. You might find all you want in a couple of days, two or three weeks, or over several months. Even if you have discovered little or nothing at all, this does not necessarily mean that the case is closed. Perhaps five years hence, you will come across an article in a magazine about a long-forgotten artist, who turns out to be the painter of your watercolour, or you might meet someone whose suggestions about your piece of furniture open up a whole new line of enquiry. 'Often the greatest discoveries are made by chance,' says renowned London dealer Anthony Mould, whose art detective talents have unmasked works by Gainsborough and Turner, among others. 'I sometimes expect to keep a picture for five or even ten years before finding a solution.' Mould itemises the qualities needed by a professional dealer/art researcher as: 'instinct, knowledge, perseverance, and luck'.

As an amateur art detective, you might not have instinct, or have had the chance to accrue knowledge, but through perseverance you can make your own luck. The more people you ask, and the more clues you follow up, the better your chance of resolving your case.

★

SAMPLE CATALOGUE ENTRY

1. Full-length portrait of Lord Important (1759–1829)
2. By Sir Joshua Painter R.A. (1769–1830) – biographical account of artist photocopied from *Dictionary of Artists*
3. Signed with the monogram JP on bottom right
4. Painted in 1805
5. English
6. Oil on canvas
7. 94 in × 57.5 in (238.8 cm × 146.1 cm)
8. Commissioned by Lord Important in 1805 and in the family's possession until sold at Christie's, 10 June 1932 (lot 41). Purchased by Mr Everyman, my grandfather, and by family descent to myself. (Biographical account of Lord Important photocopied from the *Dictionary of National*

Biography; two photocopied articles about Lord Important's family house and collection, published in *Country Life*, 26 July 1910 and 9 November 1979.)

9. Exhibited at the Royal Academy in 1805 (no. 53)

10. Discussed and illustrated in *Joshua Painter: His Life and Art*, by H. S. Tree, London, 1911, page 260, plate 59

11. In 1792, the eminent statesman and diplomat Lord Important commissioned Joshua Painter to paint his portrait. According to the artist's diary (preserved at the library of the Royal Academy, London – see photocopied pages), sittings took place at the artist's London studio on 2, 3 and 4 February, and the final portrait cost 45 guineas. The pose is identical to that of Painter's portrait of Baron Famous painted that same year. A copy of the portrait is to be found in a Scottish private collection.

12. Valuation from Sotheby's: 9 December 1991 – £18,000

To this description you could add anything that seems applicable: interesting comments about Lord Important's character made by his contemporaries; reviews of the picture when it was exhibited; a period account of Sir Joshua's portrait-painting technique, followed by an assessment of his talents from an article by a modern-day art historian. Once you have compiled the basic factual details, it is up to you how much more information you wish to uncover and include.

★

III. WHAT TO DO WITH YOUR RESEARCH

Whatever information you find, make sure you organise it clearly and keep everything together in a file, not forgetting to include a photograph of the object. Such comprehensive documentation is obviously useful for insurance purposes and could be an added advantage should you decide to sell your object.

If you have uncovered anything new or interesting, you might wish to share the fruits of your investigations. If, for example, you have gathered together material about a local artist or craftsman, pass it on to the relevant county record office where you began your research. If you think that any of the institutions you have used might be interested in your findings, send them a photocopy. Ultimately, the more information that is passed round and made freely available, the better for everybody, especially any future art detectives. Do be careful, however, not to include anything that anybody has specifically asked you to keep quiet. The term 'Private Collection' that you come across continually in catalogues and monographs means just that. You might have found out, in the course of your research, that Mr and Mrs X have a Rembrandt or a fine display of Sèvres, but for very good reasons they might not want the world to know about it. So where necessary, be discreet, particularly if you ever become involved in any professional art detecting.

You might want to write a letter about your discoveries to an appropriate magazine or journal, or possibly even an article. If the latter, contact the editorial department of the publication. In my experience as an occasional freelance journalist, I have found that it is a good idea to phone first, then, if they sound at all interested, to follow up the call with an explanatory letter. Do not be shy about speaking to editors: the worst they can say is no, which while disappointing is rarely lethal; if your story is good enough, they could well say yes. If you have never written an article before, get a literate friend to read it through first, to check for mistakes, sentences that are unclear, and so on. Even Sherlock Holmes had his Watson, and a second pair of eyes is invaluable if you are considering any form of publishable writing.

IV. LOOKING AFTER YOUR OBJECT: RESTORATION, INSURANCE AND VALUATION

RESTORATION

There are many books around that give comprehensive advice on the day-to-day care and conservation of your object, whatever it might be. However, any restoration should always be carried out by experts. To find recommended restorers working in your desired field, contact:

The Conservation Unit
Museum & Galleries Commission
16 Queen Anne's Gate
London SW1H 9AA
Tel: 071 233 3683

The United Kingdom Institute for Conservation
British Antique Furniture Restorers' Association
37 Upper Addison Gardens
London W14 8AJ
Tel: 071 603 5643

Many museums also have conservation departments that
might be able to help with suggestions.

INSURANCE
Should you require an insurance firm specialising in the fine
and decorative arts, contact the major auction houses, or
general antiques trade bodies such as BADA or LAPADA.
Any of these should be able to come up with one or two
suggestions.

VALUATION
If you want a valuation, go to an auction house or a good
dealer. From the former and often the latter, an on-the-spot
verbal valuation will be free. If you require a written valuation, expect some form of charge. Generally speaking, an
expert will calculate his or her fee either on a time basis or as
a percentage of the total value of the objects assessed. Make
sure you establish terms, costs and conditions before commit-
ting yourself.

If you are considering selling your object, get two or three
independent valuations as you would do with anything else.
Finally, remember that a valuation is only an approximate
judgement of the current market value of an object. This
market fluctuates according to changes in the economic cli-
mate, the whims of fashion, the desires of individual buyers,
and a host of other variables. However informed a valuation

might be, it is not inscribed on a tablet of stone, and every day at auction objects fetch both more and less than was reasonably estimated.

7

Additional Information and General Clues

I. HERALDRY

Coats of arms and crests can be very helpful in investigating a work of art. They appear on everything from paintings to porcelain. Not only can they tell you to which family the piece belonged, but also, in certain cases, to which individual. Heraldry thus can provide an invaluable and precise means of dating an object or painting, as well as resolving the question of provenance.

Heraldry is a language. If you know your mullets from your martlets, this is fine, but if you thought that piles and fesses were terms more suited to a medical dictionary than an armorial shield, beware. Furthermore, even if you understand the laws governing English and Scottish heraldry, you can still be floored by Continental heraldry and all those tiny European principalities which gave out coats of arms like Smarties.

If you know the name of the family to which your coat of arms belongs, then you should be able to trace it through publications such as *Burke's Peerage, Boutell's Heraldry*, and other volumes that you will find in the genealogical section of any good reference library (see page 52 for a recommended bibliography). If you have no idea to whom the arms belong, and no expertise in the field, then I would suggest seeking advice.

EXPERT WITNESSES
If your local reference library cannot help you, it is worth obtaining professional help from the following sources. Though in many cases you will be charged a fee, expert assistance will save you both time and trouble. Furthermore, if the identified crest helps to establish the provenance and date of your object, both its value and interest can be significantly increased.

England, Wales and Ireland

College of Arms
Queen Victoria Street
London EC4V 4BT
Tel: 071 248 2762
Mon–Fri: 10–4

The College of Arms in London is responsible for all aspects of English and Welsh heraldry, as well as for much of Irish and Commonwealth heraldry. Objects or photographs can be brought in for the Herald to identify, but ring to make an appointment. Though most of their material deals with English heraldry, the College also offers a limited service in identifying Continental coats of arms. A fee is charged.

Scotland

Court of the Lord Lyon
HM New Register House
Edinburgh EH1 3YT
Tel: 031 556 7255
Mon–Fri: 10–12.30, 2–4

The Lord Lyon is responsible for all Scottish heraldry and genealogy. Objects and photographs can be sent or taken in for identification, but please ring to make an appointment. Easy examples can be identified free of charge but there is a fee for more complex pieces.

Ireland
The Chief Herald of Ireland
Genealogical Office
2 Kildare Street
Dublin
Tel: 010 353 1 614877

Heraldry General

Peter de V. B. Dewar, Heraldry Consultant to Christie's, provides a private genealogical and heraldic research service. For a fee, he will identify coats of arms, crests and coronets, as well as uniforms, orders and decorations. He specialises in identifying the arms on works of art, and covers both British and foreign heraldry.

Peter de V. B. Dewar
45 Airedale Avenue
Chiswick
London W4 2NW
Tel: 081 995 6770

Specialist Library

The Society of Genealogists Library
14 Charterhouse Buildings
London EC1M 7AN
Tel: 071 251 8799
Tues, Fri, Sat: 10–6; Weds, Thurs: 10–8
Non-members: £2.50

Bibliography

GENERAL

Currer-Briggs, Noel. *World-wide Family Historian*, Oxford, Routledge, 1982

Gayre of Gayre and Nigg. *The Armorial Who's Who*, Edinburgh, 1980

Pine, L. G. *International Heraldry*, Newton Abbot, David & Charles, 1970

Von Volborth, C. A. *Heraldry of the World*, Poole, Blandford Press, 1973

UNITED KINGDOM

An Ordinary of Arms 1902–73, Edinburgh, Court of the Lord Lyon, 1977

Brooke-Little, J. P. (ed). *Boutell's Heraldry*, 9th rev ed, London, Frederick Warne, 1983

Burke, Sir B. *General Armory of England, Scotland, Ireland and Wales*, London, Burke's Peerage, 1984

Butters, Lawrence (ed). *James Fairbairn's Crests of the Families of Great Britain and Ireland*, Tokyo, Tuttle, 1968

Humphery-Smith, Cecil R. (ed). *Burke's General Armory Two: Additions and Corrections to Burke's "General Armory"*, London, Tabard Press/Heraldry Today, 1973

Innes of Learney, Sir T. *Scots Heraldry*, London, Oliver & Boyd, 1978

Papworth, J. W. and Morant, A. W. *Ordinary of British Armorials*, Trowbridge, Five Barrows, 1977 (reproduced from the original edition of 1874)

II. PATENTS AND REGISTRATION MARKS

PATENTS

Patents can be useful if you want to trace the origins of a particular design or invention. Since the late sixteenth century, the Crown has granted inventors protection for a limited period over their exclusive right to manufacture their inventions. Two principal types of document resulted: letters patent, constituting legal protection; and specifications describing the invention in more detail. The latter can be particularly revealing to the art detective, since in many cases they include plans or drawings.

Until 1853 patents and specifications for inventions were recorded in one of the three Chancery Offices, and thereafter at the Patent Office. The Public Record Office holds patents and specifications of inventions only to 1853.

Public Record Office
Ruskin Avenue
Kew
Richmond
Surrey TW9 4DU
Tel: 081 876 3444 ext 2350
Mon–Fri: 9.30–5

Photocopies of patents and specifications since 1853 may be obtained from:

Patent Office Sales Branch
Unit 6
Nine Mile Point
Cwmfelinfach
Cross Keys
Newport NP1 7HZ
Tel: 0633 246161

Printed copies of patents since 1717 are available at:

The British Library
Science Reference Library and Information Service
25 Southampton Buildings
London WC2A 1AX
Tel: 071 323 7919

★also see: National Museum of Science (page 147)

Before visiting either the Public Record Office or the Science Reference Library, it is a good idea to phone their information desk for advice and to ensure that they are the right place to answer your enquiry.

REGISTRATION MARKS

Registration numbers are a useful source of investigation, and can help you uncover not only the date of the object, but also, frequently, the maker.

In 1842 the Design Act introduced protection for those manufacturers who registered their designs with the Patent Office Design Registry in London. Designs were divided into thirteen categories and numbered (in Roman numerals):

I   Metal
II   Wood
III   Glass
IV   Earthenware (ceramics)
V   Paper Hangings
VI   Carpets

VII to XII were all various forms of textiles, while XIII included lace and miscellaneous substances not covered by the other categories.

Goods were marked, where appropriate, with a diamond-shaped registration mark giving the class of goods, the day, month and year of registration and the bundle number.

Between 1842 and 1867, the year letter appeared at the top and ran as follows:

A	1845	B	1858	C	1844
D	1852	E	1855	F	1847
G	1863	H	1843	I	1846
J	1854	K	1857	L	1856
M	1859	N	1864	O	1862
P	1851	Q	1866	R	1861
S	1849	T	1867	U	1848
V	1850	W	1865	X	1842
Y	1853	Z	1860		

From 1868 to 1883 the diamond was changed so that the year letter appeared on the right.

A	1871	C	1870	D	1878
E	1881	F	1873	H	1869
I	1872	J	1880	K	1883
L	1882	P	1877	S	1875
U	1874	V	1876	X	1868
Y	1879				

The letter W was used as the year letter from 1 to 6 March 1878.

The following letters were used for the months:

A	December	H	April
B	October	I	July
C	January	K	November
D	September	M	June
E	May	R	August
G	February	W	March

The month letter R was used between 1 and 19 September 1857; the letter K was used for December 1860.

From 1 to 16 March 1878 the letter G was used for the month.

A diagram of both diamond registration marks is given below.

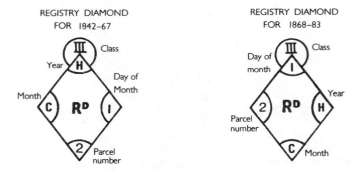

REGISTRY DIAMOND
FOR 1842–67

REGISTRY DIAMOND
FOR 1868–83

From January 1884, all categories were united in a single group and manufactured articles were marked simply with a registration number, sometimes accompanied by the prefix Reg No or Rᴅ Nᴏ, beginning logically enough with number 1. By 1890, numbers were over 140,000, and by 1900, over 350,000.

If you trace the numbers, they will give you the date of registration for the design and, in many instances, will enable you to identify the name of the manufacturer. Records are held by the Public Record Office in Kew.

PART TWO

Specific
Investigations

8
Pictures

I. EXAMINE THE EVIDENCE

First examine the evidence and look carefully at your picture. See if you can establish what medium it is in: oil, watercolour, pencil, print. This is very important: I have seen people take their cherished Old Masters to auction houses only to be told by a young man in an irreproachable grey suit: 'You do realise, of course, that this is only a photograph, not a painting.'

Having established that your work of art does not come courtesy of Kodak, examine both the front and back of the picture for a signature and a date. If there is nothing on the front, and if you cannot see the back of the picture, it is worth taking it out of its frame. If this looks at all difficult, do not do it yourself but go to a good antique dealer, a framer, or someone who is used to handling pictures (see page 79).

Copy down anything and everything you find, including inscriptions, exhibition labels, stock numbers, and the framer's sticker if it looks old. With works on paper, look for a watermark, which can sometimes yield helpful information for origins and dating, and take note of any other marks or stamps. Serious collectors often marked prints and drawings with their initials or a monogram, known as the collectors' mark, which generally can be found on the edge or reverse of the paper.

Beware of plaques on elaborate gilt frames which claim that a painting is by Gainsborough, Reynolds or some other famous artist. What these impressive little labels often fail to mention is that the work is only a reproduction of the painter's work. In general, maintain a healthy scepticism about whatever information you might find, and contain your excitement and any anticipatory spending sprees until authorship has been proved.

Write down the subject matter of the picture and take note of any interesting details of landscape, architecture or costume. This will help clarify the work in your own mind and might give you some clues as to what to look for later.

Measure the work in both inches and centimetres, and photograph it. Write down the provenance and gather together any related documentation: letters, sale catalogues, bills.

Once you have examined your work and collected all supporting evidence, you are ready to begin your research.

★

Exhibition Labels

If you find an exhibition label, you might well be able to track down the original exhibition catalogue. The V&A National Art Library has a major collection of catalogues; other good sources include the British Library and the Tate Gallery Library. If the gallery referred to still exists, contact them to see if they have kept any records pertaining to your picture.

Stock Numbers

If the painting has gone through an auction house at any stage, then the back might well be marked with a stock number and might be accompanied by a sale date and a lot number. For many years, Christie's have stamped all paintings with a stencilled combination of letters and numbers that refer to the vendor and the date of sale. This can be very helpful, because if you find such a stencil, staff at the auction house should be able to decipher it and give you such information as is permitted. Alongside the stencil,

Christie's also use chalk marks. 'If the chalk marks include no sale dates but rather a capital "N", beware,' warns art historian and former Christie's cataloguer Huon Mallalieu,† 'since this means that it was not considered to be of sufficient value to be worth offering. Equally, if there are several dates covering a short period, be cautious. The picture may have failed to sell on one or more occasion.'

Christie's is the only house to use a permanent marking system. Sotheby's numbers are written in chalk or on sticky labels about one inch (2.5 cm) in length, while Phillips often use blue chalk. Dealers also leave stock numbers behind that, when accompanied by their name, you might be able to trace in the gallery records.

Watermarks
A watermark can help to establish the period and perhaps other background details of a work. A useful guide to the subject is W. A. Churchill's *Watermarks in Paper* (1935) and for the study of paper itself, Dard Hunter's *Papermaking: The History and Technique of an Ancient Craft* (London, Dover Publications, 1978).

Collectors' Marks
The standard work on the identification of collectors' marks is F. Lugt's *Les Marques de Collections de Dessins et d'Estampes* (1921, 1956).

★

✍ II. THE INVESTIGATION

If you have not found a signature and if you have no immediate clues to follow up, turn straight to the museums and miscellaneous sources section. Let us assume for the moment, however, that you have discovered a name on your picture. It is not a painter you are familiar with nor, unfortunately, a Monet, a Rembrandt, or indeed any other artist

† Huon L. Mallalieu, *How to Buy Pictures* (Oxford, Phaidon Christie's, 1984), pp. 27–8. This is a very useful guide for the embryonic collector.

likely to have had a specific and generally available book devoted to him or her. The picture looks old, but you do not yet have enough information, expertise or confidence to say how old. Your first requirement, therefore, is to find out about the painter, and your first stop should be the local art history library.

📖 LIBRARY RESEARCH AND BASIC REFERENCE BOOKS

Check the subject index, just to make sure that the library holds no monographs on your artist. Next go to the art dictionaries section, which generally contains volumes kept on open display. The best book to consult is E. Benezit's *Dictionnaire des Artistes et des Sculpteurs* (Paris, 1976). This is a ten-volume biographical dictionary of artists, sculptors and engravers from the earliest times to the present day. It is international in scope and comprehensive, including not only celebrated figures, but also minor provincial painters; it is possible that your artist will be included, if only in one or two lines. Unfortunately, the dictionary is in French and has not been translated. Do not worry, however, if your French never progressed beyond the 'bonjour' standard; even if you do not fully understand the entry, you will still be able to make out the dates of the painter and the country in which he lived. For better known artists, Benezit also lists which museums have examples of their work, and what prices (in francs) their paintings have fetched at auction throughout the years.

> A lack of linguistic knowledge can lead to some interesting interpretations. I was wandering round a Braque exhibition with a musical friend who pointed to one picture with great excitement. 'Just look at that brilliant title,' he enthused, ' "Nature Killed by Guitar".' What he had failed to realise was that 'nature morte' was the French for still-life. A good French/English dictionary is a useful tool for the art detective.

Whether or not you have found your artist's name in Benezit, do spend some time looking through the other art dictionaries on the shelves. Among the best, particularly for British painters, are those published by the Antique Collectors' Club. Most of these dictionaries are divided by period (*Dictionary of British 18th-Century Painters*), by subject matter (*Dictionary of Sea Painters*) or by medium (*Dictionary of British Watercolour Artists*), which makes them particularly easy to consult. Some dictionary entries also list individual bibliographies for the artist concerned. Make sure you take note of the books and magazine articles referred to, since in trying to identify your painting you are going to need to collate as much background material as possible.

Perhaps the best source of early reference works for artists up to the turn of the century is Thieme and Becker's *Kunstler Lexicon*, a multi-volumed dictionary of artists, published in Leipzig in the first half of the century, which should be lurking ponderously on the shelves not too far from Benezit. Thieme-Becker is international, includes a wide range of artists, and is another masterwork that has not been translated, in this case from its original German. Again it does not matter, if you do not read the language, as you are using this book simply as a stepping stone for other sources of reference. You will be able to understand dates and proper names, and at the foot of each entry is a bibliography, sometimes an extensive one, listing books and articles in which the artist has appeared, along with the relevant page numbers. The titles of these works are in their native language, and at least the numbers are international.

Staying in the dictionary section, if your artist is British, check the lists of Royal Academy exhibitors. In the past, as today, the annual summer exhibitions at the Academy included a wide range of contributors encompassing both fine artists and enthusiastic amateurs of the puppy and kitten school of painting. The volumes cited below include all of the artists, the titles of their various works and the years in which they were shown. Who knows, you might even find your own picture included among the lists.

Royal Academy Exhibitors, 1905–70: A Complete Dictionary, Calne, Wilts, Hilmarton Manor Press, 1986

Graves, Algernon. *Royal Academy of Arts: A Complete*

Dictionary of Contributors and Their Work from its Foundation in 1769 to 1904, Bath, Kingsmead Press, 1970
Laperriere, Charles Baile de (ed). *Royal Academy Exhibitors, 1971–89*. Calne, Wilts, Hilmarton Manor Press, 1989.

Do take time to go through the dictionaries on the open shelves and to familiarise yourself with their contents. Though your local library might only have a standard collection, at major libraries you will find a vast selection of different art dictionaries specialising in everything from French flower painters to Northumberland artists. Another useful source of information is the *Dictionary of National Biography*, and many countries have produced similar publications – available at major libraries – if you are researching foreign figures. See page 23 for further biographical information.

Having gathered together as much material as you can from all these basic reference books, I would recommend that you go home. Do not try and absorb too much at once. Far better to stop, take stock of the information that you have gathered, and plan your next move.

Bibliography

The books referred to above are predominantly dictionaries of artists. Though the subject is too broad for a detailed bibliography, the following works which deal with prints and watercolours are recommended.

Print Bibliography

In order to investigate and identify your print, you will need to have some understanding of the different printmaking techniques. Helpful and accessible introductions to the subject are provided by Bamber Gascoigne in *How to Identify Prints: Complete Guide to Manual and Mechanical Processes from Woodcut to Ink Jet* (London, Thames & Hudson, 1987), and by Antony Griffiths in *Prints and Printmaking, An Introduction to the History and Techniques* (London, British Museum Publications, 1980).

Print Catalogues

There are any number of print catalogues, ranging from

the general works covering whole schools to specific mono-graphs on individual artists. The print bible and perhaps the greatest catalogue ever compiled in the field is Adam Bartsch's *Le Peintre-Graveur* (21 vols, Vienna, 1803–1821). This treats the work of printmakers active before 1700, and covers Dutch, Flemish, German and Italian engravers. A number of supplements were added later by other experts, extending the range of the work.

For an introduction to this and other standard catalogues of prints see A. Griffiths, pages 128–31. For specialist advice, one of the best places to consult is the Print Room at the British Museum (see page 72).

Watercolour Bibliography

Many volumes have been published about British water-colours. Among the finest is Martin Hardie's *Watercolour Painting in Britain*, 3 vols. (London, B. T. Batsford Ltd, 1966–8). This covers its subject from the eighteenth century to the Victorian age, and includes an extensive bibliography.

📖 FURTHER ENQUIRIES AND SPECIALIST LIBRARIES

If all has gone according to plan, you might now have some basic details about your artist: a short biography and some dates. You still know nothing about the picture itself, and little about the painter's work in general. If your artist is not famous enough to have had any books written about him or her, which is more than likely, you are going to have to dig up your own information from magazines, sale catalogues and archives.

One of the principal rules of research is always to make it as easy for yourself as you can and, where possible, to take full advantage of all available resources. You don't want to spend ages tracking down references in esoteric tomes if somebody has already done some of the work for you, and in the hope of this, I would suggest a trip to London.

The Witt Library (and Conway Library)
Courtauld Institute of Art
Somerset House
Strand
London WC2 0RN
Tel: 071 873 2777 (reception)

Mon–Fri: 10–7 (term time), 10–6 (vacation), closed ten days at Christmas and Easter, and two weeks in August or September for stocktaking.

Your first port of call should be the Witt Library, part of the Courtauld Institute, perhaps the most famous college in Britain for degrees in art history. The Witt, which is open to the general public, is a picture library, and an absolutely invaluable source of reference.

The library consists of photographs and reproductions of works by Western artists from *circa* 1200 to the present day. The material is stored in box-files on open-access shelves, and divided into national schools organised alphabetically by artist. These box-files, the result of years of an assiduous collecting of photographs and clipping from magazines and catalogues, provide a marvellously detailed portfolio of an artist's works, including paintings, copies, studies, drawings and prints. Therefore, you might not only be able to find further examples of your artist's oeuvres, but if you are extremely lucky, you could even come across a reproduction of your own picture, or perhaps a drawing related to it.

The Witt Collection can tell you many things. If you are researching a sketch by artist X, for example, it is worth not only looking through X's drawings, but also his paintings to see if perhaps your piece was originally a study for some larger canvas. You might find that your apparently original work of art is, in fact, one of several almost indistinguishable copies. In the past it was not unknown for an artist and his studio to produce numerous versions of his more successful works.

I once researched a portrait of George IV, in his garter robes, by Sir Thomas Lawrence. The artist, who clearly knew when he was on to a good thing, produced some fourteen replicas of this painting and, as irate clients noticed, occasionally charged as much and even more for a copy than for the original picture. This is where it is very important to have the measurements of your painting written down, because sometimes it is only the size that allows you to distinguish between two seemingly identical works.

Frequently, a box-file will contain several reproductions of the same picture, thus enabling you to trace its history throughout the years. For example, there might be a photograph of a painting by artist X in an article about Lord Y's collection, written in 1900. Twenty years later, Lord Y died, and his family put his paintings up for auction. Thus the picture makes its second appearance at the Witt, this time as an illustration in the sale catalogue. It is purchased by Mr Z III, a wealthy American businessman, who subsequently lends the painting to an exhibition. It is illustrated in the exhibition catalogue and finds its way into the collection for a third time.

Remember that when you are researching a picture, the history of who owned the work – the provenance – can sometimes be nearly as important as who painted it. Social snobbery is as much a fact of art research as it is of life: a good provenance not only confirms the authenticity of a picture, but can also, if sufficiently star-studded or interesting, significantly increase its value.

The Witt is very useful for provenance details, since the extracts from catalogues and articles can often provide much information about the painting and its owners. It will also add to your increasing bibliography.

The library keeps a small selection of standard reference books (Benezit, Thieme-Becker, etc) for public use, and has also compiled a number of different indexes to the main collection (British Portraits 1680–1780, Master and Pupil Index).

Upstairs from the Witt is the Conway Library, which, although considerably smaller, fulfils a similar function for sculpture, architecture, and certain other subjects. The Conway also holds the Garisson Collection, a resource for the study of Italian medieval painting that includes photographs and a small reference library.

Finally, on a more mundane note, the library has good photocopying facilities and a change machine.

The Witt can provide you with references to published works which you can then track down in the library (see chapter 3 for further details). For finding archives and unpublished material, refer to chapter 4. The Royal Commission on Historical Manuscripts is only a short walk away from the Witt, so it is a good idea to kill two birds with one stone and visit both institutions on the same day.

✍ III. EXPERT WITNESSES: MUSEUMS AND MISCELLANEOUS SOURCES

If you have not got a clue about your picture, or if having tracked down the basic evidence you now need further help, you should seek the assistance of an expert witness.

The art of obtaining good specialist advice lies in finding the right person to ask. This is largely common sense: if you are investigating a marine painting, you should go to a maritime museum; a portrait, try the National Portrait Gallery. When working on a particular painter, look for a place that specialises in his oeuvre; if your artist is from a regional school, contact the relevant local museum.

The same process applies to researching the pictorial elements of a painting. If you want help with dating a lady's dress, go to the Costume Department at the V&A; to name the blooms in your flower painting, consult the Natural History Museum; to identify a painted Oriental rug on a table, ask a carpet expert. Look carefully at your picture and allow it to point you in the right direction.

Listed below is an abbreviated selection of museums to which you can turn for advice; in some cases they also have library facilities and archives. As well as museums covering the subject in general, I have picked out certain collections specialising in works of a particular type or school, and have included related societies and libraries. See the Appendix for addresses and opening times.

🏛 MUSEUMS
London

ARCHITECTURAL DRAWINGS
Royal Institute of British Architects
Drawings Collection

The collection comprises some 400,000 drawings, and includes works by architects such as Palladio, Inigo Jones, C. A. Voysey, and Sir Edwin Lutyens. Viewing is by appointment only, and it is advisable to telephone or write beforehand to see if the collection or staff can help you with your enquiry.

Royal Institute of British Architects
British Architectural Library

Most of the library's material relates to the lives and works of British architects, though designers, craftsmen, painters and sculptors also feature in the collection. The library is open to the public; no appointment is necessary.

Sir John Soane's Museum

Amid a fine collection that includes paintings and engravings by Hogarth, English neo-classical sculpture, furniture and pictures, the museum houses a major collection of architectural drawings from the Italian Renaissance to the early nineteenth century. The research library (open by appointment Tues–Fri: 10–1, 2–5; Sat: 10–1) contains some 40,000 architectural drawings, including 8,000 from the studio of Robert Adam, the archive of Sir John Soane and many architectural books. The Librarian recommends that researchers with enquiries about Soane should first consult the standard biography of the architect, *Sir John Soane, Architect*, written by Dorothy Stroud (London, Faber & Faber, 1984). Consultations are available by appointment and by post.

ART GENERAL
National Gallery

The gallery's collection covers Western European painting from the thirteenth to the early twentieth centuries. Paintings falling into this category may be brought in for identification or advice from a curator on Wednesday afternoons, 2.30–5. Postal enquiries are preferred.

The Victoria & Albert Museum

The Prints and Drawings Department offers an opinion service on Tuesday afternoons, 2.30–4.30. The Print Room is open Tues–Fri: 10–4.30; Sat: 10–1 and 2–4.30.

BRITISH ART GENERAL, TWENTIETH CENTURY ART
WORLDWIDE
Tate Gallery

The Tate Gallery houses the national collection of British painting and twentieth-century painting and sculpture. The museum's archives include documentary material relating to twentieth-century British art and artists, along with some foreign and some earlier material. The library covers British art from the Renaissance onwards, and twentieth-century art worldwide. It is available for reference use, by appointment only, to researchers unable to locate the material they require elsewhere. The Tate has no consultation days, but if you write to them with an enquiry, they will endeavour to put you in touch with the relevant expert.

ENGLISH WATERCOLOURS
Royal Society of Painters-Printmakers (formerly Royal Society of Painters, Etchers and Engravers, founded 1880)
Royal Watercolour Society (founded 1804)

Bankside Gallery is the home and exhibition centre for these two societies. The library (open by appointment) holds a major archive connected with nineteenth-century watercolour painting, including the catalogues and sales books of the societies from their foundation onwards, artists' letters, and Joseph John Jenkins' papers relating to J. L. Roget's *History of the Old Watercolour Society*. At present, there is a researcher employed one day a week who can help with enquiries.

LONDON MATERIAL
Guildhall Library and Print Room

The Guildhall Library specialises in printed books, archives, prints, drawings, and maps relating to London. It is a good place for researching topographical studies of London, London artists and subjects connected with the city. The library has collated a major archive concerning portraits of the Lord Mayor throughout the centuries; and the drawings collection includes over 200 drawings from the office of Sir Christopher Wren. Other important material held by the Print Room includes an unrivalled collection of London maps, satirical prints, panoramas, and prints relating to social themes. It holds some 16,000 portraits and houses the Willshire Collection of Old Master Prints.

MARINE PICTURES AND MARITIME SUBJECT MATTER
National Maritime Museum

The museum's superb art collection includes the largest group of seventeenth-century Dutch marine paintings in the world, a major portrait collection, and a comprehensive range of paintings related to the sea and its history. The Print Room houses a huge display of maritime prints and drawings, as well as historic photographs. Consultations are given by appointment, and in my experience the staff are both welcoming and wonderfully informed. The library, which covers maritime history in its largest sense, is open to the public Mon–Fri: 10–4.45; Sat: by prior arrangement only.

NATURAL HISTORY PAINTING, PRINTS AND ILLUSTRATION
Natural History Museum
The libraries of the Natural History Museum hold 375,000 original watercolour natural history paintings, an important print collection and are a major source of information on natural history art and illustration in all its forms.

PORTRAITS
National Portrait Gallery and NPG Archive and Library
The gallery houses a remarkable display of portraits of famous British men and women. The archive is extremely useful in that it extends well beyond the museum's own collection, including some 500,000 engravings and photographic reproductions of British portraits arranged by artist and sitter. Therefore, if you look under Sir Walter Raleigh, for example, you can find reproductions of all his known portraits, engravings, etc. This form of cataloguing can be extremely helpful if you are researching the portrait of a public figure.

There is an important archive of portrait photographs, and the library contains some 30,000 books, as well as special collection material such as artists' sitter books and Gillray caricatures. Opinions and identifications are given, by appointment only, at the archive in Lewisham.

Royal College of Music
As well as housing a museum of musical instruments, the Royal College has a department of portraits containing several thousand prints, photographs and paintings of musicians. Consultations are available by appointment. The college's library is open to the public, Mon–Fri: 10.30–5.

NB: With portraits, generally allow the identity of the sitter to point you in the right direction. If the picture shows an admiral, try the National Maritime Museum (see page 71). For a theatrical figure, perhaps the Theatre Museum (see page 206) will be able to help with your enquiries. Many museums house portrait collections that are relevant to their specific field.

PRINTS AND DRAWINGS
The British Museum
Department of Prints and Drawings

The British Museum houses one of the world's most important collections of prints and drawings, containing over two million items. It was built up as a reference collection to enable students to follow the history and development of graphic art from its beginnings up to the present day. For the art detective, it can provide an invaluable source of reference, and it is probably the best place in Britain to go for initial advice about a drawing or print. A free opinion service is offered every afternoon between 2.15 and 4. To consult the collection and to examine the prints and drawings, you will need to collect and fill in an application form, which must also be signed by a referee: 'a person of recognised position who can be identified from the ordinary sources of reference and who is not related to the applicant' (i.e. someone who sounds responsible and who knows you reasonably well).

It is impossible to summarise the riches of a collection which is strong in so many areas: Old Master prints and drawings, works by the British School, topographical studies, a magnificent display of political and personal satires, etc. For advice on using the collection see A. Griffiths and R. Williams, *The Department of Prints and Drawings in the British Museum: User's Guide* (London, British Museum Publications, 1987). Much of the collection has also been catalogued, and you will find the catalogues in any good art history library.

ROYAL ACADEMY
Royal Academy Library

The library of the Royal Academy specialises in eighteenth- and nineteenth–century British art. As well as much published material, it holds archives, letters and papers concerning Royal

Academicians and Associate Members. This is not a place to take your painting for an instant identification, but if you are researching the works of a Royal Academy painter or sculptor, its material – particularly the letter books of artists such as John Gibson, Ozias Humphry, and Sir Thomas Lawrence – can provide a treasure trove of information. The staff will answer postal enquiries, but you should try to be very specific about what you want.

Regional

ART GENERAL AND LIVERPOOL ARTISTS
Walker Art Gallery, Liverpool

The museum houses a fine general collection of British and European painting and decorative arts. Particular strengths include early Italian and Netherlandish works, and British paintings of the eighteenth and nineteenth centuries. There is a section devoted to artists of the Liverpool School. The museum library is open by appointment; archives include the records of the Liverpool Academy. Consultations are given on Thursday afternoons, 2–4.

ART GENERAL AND PRINTS
Ashmolean Museum, Oxford

The museum's Western Art Department houses one of the world's major print rooms, which incorporates works by Raphael, Michelangelo and Rembrandt, among others. There is a fine collection of both British and European paintings, and papers held include the Pissarro Archive and some important Pre-Raphaelite material. Consultations are provided on Wednesday afternoons and by post.

Fitzwilliam Museum, Cambridge

The museum's collection contains Western European paintings, drawings and prints from the fourteenth century to the present day. Consultations are available by appointment.

BRIGHTON ARTISTS, BRITISH ART, TWENTIETH CENTURY
Hove Museum and Art Gallery

The museum specialises in twentieth-century British paintings and drawings. There is a strong emphasis on local pictures; the museum also holds the archives of Brighton Arts Club, 1910–1960. Consultations are available by appointment and by post.

BRITISH ART, NINETEENTH AND TWENTIETH CENTURY
Wolverhampton Art Gallery and Museum

The museum specialises in twentieth-century British art, and also holds a good collection of Victorian genre paintings, specifically works by the Cranbrook Colony artists. The reference library can be opened by arrangement, and archives include the papers of sculptor R. J. Emerson. Consultations are available by appointment.

BRITISH ART, PRE-RAPHAELITE PAINTING
Manchester City Art Gallery

The gallery has a large collection of British art, especially from the nineteenth century. The Pre-Raphaelite collection is claimed to be the finest in public ownership, and includes letters, papers and memorabilia, as well as paintings and drawings. An opinion service is available on Wednesdays, 2–4.

BRITISH ART, TWENTIETH CENTURY
Graves Art Gallery, Sheffield

The gallery specialises in twentieth-century British art. A picture opinion service is available on Wednesdays, 12–2.

BRITISH AND EUROPEAN ART, NINETEENTH AND TWENTIETH CENTURY
Leeds City Art Gallery

The gallery's holdings include a fine collection of Romantic British watercolours, twentieth-century British paintings, particularly those of the Camden Town Group, and works by turn of the century French artists. It also houses the Kitson Bequest of 750 pencil sketches by J. S. Cotman.

The Henry Moore Centre for the Study of Sculpture, which is at present building up a major archive collection on the history of British sculpture, is based at the gallery. Its holdings include material related to Hamo Thorneycroft, a nineteenth-century sculptor, and photographic archives on Jacob Epstein and Eric Gill. Identifications are made by appointment and by post. Please give advance notice before coming to consult the collection.

BRITISH WATERCOLOURS, PRINTS AND ART GENERAL
Whitworth Art Gallery, Manchester

CARTOON AND CARICATURE
The Centre for the Study of Cartoon and Caricature

Kent University holds a research archive of twentieth-century original cartoon drawings for newspapers and magazines, comprising some 70,000 works. There is a small reference library and the centre keeps some biographical material pertaining to the artists. Consultations and visits are available by appointment.

For those interested in cartoons and caricatures from the eighteenth century onwards, the Cartoon Art Trust is planning to establish a museum devoted to British cartoon art and could be a useful source of advice.

The Cartoon Art Trust
19 Erlington Road
London E8 3BJ
Tel: 071 241 6950

CHESHIRE ARTISTS
Grosvenor Museum, Chester

DEVON ARTISTS
Royal Albert Memorial Museum, Exeter

The main emphasis of the collection is British art, with a large selection of works by Devon-born and associated artists, and it also has a good representation of local topography. There is a small but sound departmental library that can be consulted by the researcher. Identifications can be made and enquiries answered by appointment and by post. The museum requests that topographical and genealogical enquiries should not be addressed to them but to the West Country Studies Library or Devon Records Office.

GLOUCESTERSHIRE ARTISTS
Cheltenham Art Gallery and Museum

LANCASTER ARTISTS
Lancaster City Museum

The museum specialises in the arts and crafts connected with the area, and the collection is particularly strong in works by local artists. Archives include detailed information on local artists, and the museum's library can be consulted by appointment.

LIVERPOOL ARTISTS
See Art General and Liverpool Artists

MARINE PAINTING, HUMBERSIDE MARINE ARTISTS
Ferens Art Gallery and Town Docks Museum, Hull

The museum specialises in Humberside marine artists, and related archives can be consulted by arrangement. Consultations are available by appointment or by post.

NORTH–EAST AND NEWCASTLE PAINTINGS
Laing Art Gallery, Newcastle–upon–Tyne

The gallery's focus is on North-East and Newcastle paintings, and its archives relate to local artists. Consultations are available by appointment.

NORWICH SCHOOL
Norwich Castle Museum

The museum specialises in the Norwich School of artists, and their records may be examined by appointment. Consultations for all subjects covered by the museum are held on Wednesdays. The museum also offers a free public enquiry service, whereby objects may be left at the museum for a written identification (phone for details).

SUNDERLAND ARTISTS
Sunderland Museum and Art Gallery

YORKSHIRE ARTISTS
Darlington Art Gallery

The museum has a good collection of work by early twentieth-century Yorkshire artists. It does not have archives or a library, but the public reference library is housed in the same building. Consultations are available by appointment and by post.

Northern Ireland

ART GENERAL AND IRISH ARTISTS
Ulster Museum, Belfast

Republic of Ireland

ART GENERAL AND IRISH ARTISTS
The Hugh Lane Municipal Gallery of Modern Art, Dublin
This gallery houses important collections of nineteenth- and twentieth-century European and Irish art. Consultations are available by appointment.

The National Gallery of Ireland, Dublin
The gallery covers European painting from the Renaissance to the twentieth century, and includes an important display of Irish work, sculpture (a major collection), prints, drawings, watercolours and miniatures. It is also home to the National Portrait Collection. Consultations are available by appointment.

Scotland

ART GENERAL AND SCOTTISH ARTISTS
Hunterian Art Gallery, Glasgow
The collection specialises in Scottish paintings of the nineteenth and twentieth centuries, the work of painter James McNeill Whistler and designer Charles Rennie Mackintosh, and European prints. The gallery holds archives concerning Mackintosh, and the library is open by written appointment for those researching Whistler or Mackintosh.

National Gallery of Scotland, Edinburgh
The gallery holds a collection of Old Master, French Impressionist, British and Scottish paintings, and Old Master, British and Scottish prints, drawings and watercolours. Consultations are available by appointment.

Royal Scottish Academy, Edinburgh
The library holds archives concerning the Academy and its

members from 1826 until the present day. Their material includes catalogues, annual reports, letters, sales records, files on members, and a good collection of published material on Scottish art.

Scottish National Gallery of Modern Art, Edinburgh

Twentieth-century paintings, sculpture, drawings and prints are the focus of this museum. Consultations are available by appointment. The gallery's archives include material relating to various Scottish artists; the library is open by arrangement.

Scottish National Portrait Gallery, Edinburgh

The collection covers Scottish and British portraiture and the history of photography, particularly in Scotland. The library is open to the public by appointment, and the archives include material relating to Scottish art history and photography. Consultations are available on Thursdays and by post.

Wales

ART GENERAL AND WELSH ARTISTS

Glynn Vivian Art Gallery and Museum, Swansea

The museum houses a collection of works by Welsh artists, and the library holds detailed information on the same. Consultations are available by appointment and by post.

National Library of Wales, Aberystwyth (see page 26)

The National Library of Wales is a British copyright library. It holds extensive collections of books, manuscripts, archives, maps, pictures, prints, and photographs, and a wide range of audio-visual material. The library houses the archives of numerous artists with Welsh associations, including Augustus John, Gwen John and David Jones. Readers wishing to consult original works of art are advised to make an appointment before visiting.

National Museum of Wales, Cardiff

The museum has a fine art collection, strong in Welsh artists from the eighteenth to twentieth centuries, French realist and Impressionist paintings, sculpture and British 'New Sculpture'. Opinions are given by appointment.

✐ IV. FRAMES

As a general rule, unless you know what you are doing, it is a good idea to get an expert, either an antique dealer or a good professional framer, to remove your picture from its frame. Enthusiastic and uninformed prising apart could result in damage to the painting or to the frame itself. As frame specialist John Davies notes, good antique frames have become collectable in their own right, with fine examples fetching as much as £30,000. Furthermore, adds Davies, frames can be a source of valuable information, and not only in terms of their design. Occasionally a provenance will be inscribed on the back of the wood, and sometimes a frame will bear the signature or label of its maker. If this proves to be contemporaneous with the picture, it can provide a helpful source for dating.

The structure of the frame and the way the picture is fitted into it can also reveal certain clues: if nails are square-cut, it suggests that the piece is over 100 years old, while a mitred corner at the back can indicate that a frame has been cut down, and that it was originally intended for a larger work, not for your painting.

You cannot expect to authenticate your picture solely from its surround. Frames followed the fashions of the day and would often be replaced when a painting changed hands or the owner redecorated his or her living room. Nevertheless, a frame can form part of the story of a painting, as well as being a work of art in its own right. If you have a fine example, treat it with care and, above all, do not overclean it.

📖 **BOOKS, LIBRARY RESEARCH AND SPECIALIST ADVICE**
A knowledge of furniture styles and architecture is perhaps the greatest help in dating frames, since framers followed the prevailing decorative fashions of the day. Unfortunately, comparatively little specific research has been carried out on the subject, and the greatest expertise remains in the hands of antique frame dealers, restoration experts, and those handling pictures and frames on a daily and practical basis.

Some years ago, I was trying to trace the framer's label on an early nineteenth-century stretcher in an attempt to date a problematic painting. In the restoration department of the Tate, I came across an index of period framers, complete with dates and addresses, compiled from frames that the department had seen and worked with over the years. So when consulting a museum, it might be worth trying not only the picture department, but also the restoration section, which might prove to be a better source of working knowledge in the field.

If you come across a framer's name on a label, and cannot find any reference to him in furniture or frame books, or any other sources, you will have to do your own research (see chapter 4).

Bibliography

The Art Institute of Chicago. *The Art of the Edge: European Frames 1300–1900*, Chicago, 1986
Grimm, Claus. *The Book of Picture Frames*, New York, Abaris Books, 1981

Occasionally monographs on furniture and the decorative arts will include information on frames, and there is a good introduction to the subject in Ralph Edwards (ed), *The Dictionary of English Furniture* (Woodbridge, Antique Collectors' Club, 1983).

Specialist Dealers

Arnold Wiggins and Sons Ltd
4 Bury Street
St James's
London SW1
Tel: 071 925 0195

Paul Mitchell Ltd
99 New Bond Street
London W1
Tel: 071 493 8732

John Davies Framing Ltd
8 Bury Street
St James's
London SW1
Tel: 071 930 7795

Auction houses with the most knowledgeable experts in this field are (currently) Bonhams and Christie's.

9

Sculpture

Many of the reference books and general institutions mentioned in the previous chapter are as relevant to sculpture as they are to paintings, so this section is comparatively brief and should be read in conjunction with chapter 8.

I. EXAMINE THE EVIDENCE

Begin by trying to establish what material your sculpture is made from: bronze, marble, wood, clay, etc. Measure the height, note down the subject matter, transcribe any provenance details, and take photographs, both front and rear.

Examine the work in detail. Are there any inscriptions, stamps or signatures? Note down anything you find.

When investigating a bronze, be careful not to confuse the name of the sculptor with that of the foundry which cast the work. The terms 'editeur' or 'fondeur' inscribed before a name refer to the manufacturer. If you are researching a small table bronze take note – or even a photograph – of the style of the base and turn the work over to see how it has been fixed in. Even though this will mean little to the amateur sculpture detective, for the specialist such clues can be vital when it comes to dating the object.

Remember that your cherished work of art could be one of literally dozens of identical examples, and that these bronzes could have appeared in numerous editions at any time during the artist's life or even after his death. Reproductions are legion in this field. 'I would hazard a guess that there are far more copies than original editions on the market,' says Peter Christie, dealer in nineteenth-century bronzes, with a cynicism born of twenty years in the trade.

Even if you are investigating a work in marble, this does not mean that it is necessarily a one-off. For example, the nineteenth-century portrait sculptor Sir Francis Chantrey produced at least seventeen replicas of one of his marble busts of George IV, at a healthy 200 guineas apiece. Then, as now, the fact that a work of art is not unique does not mean that it is not original, and it need not affect its value.

But as Sherlock Holmes would no doubt concur, speculation without evidence is a fairly fruitless endeavour. At this stage, all you can do is look carefully at your object and try to be aware of the different elements of structure, design and decoration. Having compiled your dossier of observations and provenance, you can then proceed to the next stage.

✎ II. THE INVESTIGATION

📖 LIBRARY RESEARCH AND BASIC REFERENCE BOOKS

For looking up the name of your sculptor, if you are lucky enough to have found one, follow the process suggested in chapter 8 and begin with the same general reference books. A short bibliography of helpful and more specific dictionaries and monographs is listed below.

Compared to paintings, sculpture is surprisingly under-researched, and there is a lack of good and comprehensive books in certain fields. You might have to sniff around a bit to dig up published clues. It is important to remember that material on sculpture can be found not only in volumes devoted to the subject, but also in books on art, architecture and the decorative arts. Exhibition catalogues and even guidebooks containing information about statues and local artists can also be of use; also, many seminal articles have been published by art magazines.

Bibliography

BRITISH

Beattie, Susan. *The New Sculpture,* London, Yale University Press, 1983

Gunnis, Robert. *Dictionary of British Sculptures, 1660–1851*, 2nd rev ed, London, Murrays Sales & Service Co, 1968

Read, B. and Skipwith, P. *Sculpture in Britain Between the Wars*, London, Fine Art Society exhibition catalogue, 1986

Read, Benedict. *Victorian Sculpture*, London, Yale University Press, 1982

Whinney, Margaret. *Sculpture in Britain 1530–1830*, London, Penguin Books, 1988

BRONZES

Cooper, J. *Nineteenth Century Romantic Bronzes*, Newton Abbot, David & Charles, 1975

Horswell, Jane (ed). *Price Guide to the Bronze Sculptures of "Les Animaliers"*, Woodbridge, Antique Collectors' Club, 1971

Kjellberg, P. *Les Bronzes du XIXe Siècle, Dictionnaire des Sculpteurs*, Paris, 1987

Makay, James Alexander. *The Dictionary of Western Sculptors in Bronze*, Woodbridge, Antique Collectors' Club, 1977

Payne, Christopher. *Animals in Bronze: Reference and Price Guide*, Woodbridge, Antique Collectors' Club, 1986

FRENCH

Lami, S. *Dictionnaire des Sculpteurs de l'Ecole Française.* A selection of volumes that covers its subject from the Middle Ages until the nineteenth century, published between 1898 and 1921.

ITALIAN

Bessone, A. *Dizionario de scultori e architetti italiani*, 1947

Pope-Hennessy, John. *Introduction to Italian Sculpture*, rev ed, 3 vols, London, Phaidon Press, 1986

📖 FURTHER ENQUIRIES AND SPECIALIST LIBRARIES

In addition to discovering the name and dates of your sculptor, there could be any number of questions you might want answered. Is the work unique or one of many identical examples? Is it a reduction of a known monumental work? Are there any drawings, models or other material that relate to it? If it is a large piece, was it designed for a particular place, and who commissioned it? Has it ever appeared in any exhibitions or catalogues? The list of questions can be, if not endless, certainly extensive, and a good place to begin your enquiries is the Conway Library and the Courtauld Institute in London.

As at the Witt (see page 65), the material at the Conway consists of a series of photographs, illustrations, etc, contained in box-files and organised by century, nationality and artist. As well as pictures from published sources, the library holds many original photographs of sculpture throughout the world. One of their more recent projects has been to photograph all of the sculpture and decorative art objects with figural content that appeared in the *Illustrated London News* from its foundation until 1900. Although the library is open daily, if you want advice or opinions from a specific librarian, it is a good idea to make an appointment to see them.

As with every other subject, local history libraries and record offices can be useful in certain circumstances. I once investigated a marble sculpture by an obscure nineteenth-century Italian sculptor. From the Conway's archives I discovered that there was a statue by the same artist in a London square. Because the work portrayed a peculiarly winsome little boy – children, like animals, are endlessly popular themes – it was much loved by local residents, who over the years had contributed little snippets of information about the artist and his work to the local history library, resulting in a whole file of useful material that I would not have been able to find elsewhere. In researching sculpture, as in every other field, explore every available avenue, since you never know what you might find.

✍ III. EXPERT WITNESSES: MUSEUMS AND MISCELLANEOUS SOURCES

Many of the museums listed in the painting section will be able to advise you on sculpture. Leeds City Art Gallery is building up a major archive on British sculpture, and other museums that have been highly recommended to me by experts in the field include the V&A, the National Museum of Wales and the National Gallery of Ireland. As usual, the auction houses and specialist dealers can also be an invaluable source of reference.

10
Furniture

Investigating furniture is somewhat different from researching pictures in that much of the time you will not be looking for a specific craftsman. Much English furniture is anonymous. It is rare to find stamped or marked pieces before the nineteenth century. There is no such thing as a Chippendale label nor has any single item ever been proved to have come from the hand of Sheraton. In the absence of any specific mark, furniture can be identified through the existence of original bills and papers, or, though this method is by no means foolproof, by comparison with designs and other authenticated pieces. With the great majority of works, however, do not expect to discover a maker; the best you can hope to find is the nationality, an approximate date, perhaps a similar example or design to relate it to, and, if you are lucky, some provenance information.

To some extent, much of the art of furniture research is a form of aesthetic patchwork. Depending on the nature of your object, you could find a related design in a contemporary pattern book, a similar piece in a country house collection, or the photograph of an almost identical work in an advertisement placed by a London dealer in a monthly art magazine. Even though these examples might not allow you to attribute your object to any specific maker or designer, they help to set the work in context.

Perhaps you have discovered that your object came from a certain country mansion: you should then examine the records of the house for inventories and bills, and look through books and magazines for further information about the building and its inhabitants. Even if you cannot find any specific reference to your piece of furniture, by assembling this material you will be able to form a picture of its historical background: the fashions that shaped it and the people who owned it.

In this field, as in all others, the art of being a good art detective lies in knowing how to make the most of other people's research and expertise (see Part One). For example, the comparison of a work with a well-researched piece in a public or private collection can prove a fascinating and ready-made source of information.

I recently investigated an eighteenth-century *bonheur-du-jour* – lady's dressing table – decorated with particularly distinctive marquetry; its owner knew nothing about it and had purchased it simply because underneath the wear and tear of centuries, he recognised its quality.

Looking through a monograph on Georgian furniture, I came across the photograph of another *bonheur-du-jour*, completely identical to my client's except for one panel bearing a family badge. This piece had been commissioned *circa* 1770 by a famous patron for one of Britain's more prestigious stately homes. It had been written about in art magazines, illustrated in seminal books, and was recognised as being an exceptional piece of furniture. What is more, a letter to the National Trust revealed that recent research had enabled the piece to be attributed to John Cobb, cabinetmaker to George III.

Much to his delight, my client turned out to have its twin, undoubtedly by the same hand; his suspicion of the importance of his piece had been fully confirmed and its value was significantly enhanced. Much to my delight, I had managed to compile this information with some speed and comparatively little effort. Such satisfying conclusions to art historical mysteries might be few and far between, but they do happen.

A final point that the embryo furniture detective should be aware of is the existence of fakes and reproductions. The books that you have waded through might well show you that the design of your table is *circa* 1750, but is the table itself an original piece, a nineteenth-century copy, perhaps valuable in its own right, or a modern reproduction? Only experience or an expert can tell you this, and when in doubt consult the latter.

✍ I. EXAMINE THE EVIDENCE

Begin with the most important clue, the piece of furniture. Write down what it is, take note of the measurements, photograph it, and gather together any known provenance information.

'Begin by looking at the object as a whole,' recommends Christopher Hawkings, deputy chairman at Phillips auction house. 'Does it appear well made? Is the carving crisp? Do the proportions seem right? Does it "feel" good? Look hard and use your common sense; most people can make some assessment of quality.'

What material is the object constructed from? 'Even if you cannot identify the wood itself,' advises dealer and furniture historian Martin Levy, 'you can compile a basic description: what is the colour like, is the wood light or dark, painted or plain, is the grain simple or complex?'

Having looked at the piece as a whole, next examine it in detail to see if you can get some idea of its decorative and constructional features. With a chair, for example, what is the shape of the back like? Is the rail curved or straight? How does the seat fit – does it drop in or is it part of the frame? What shape are the legs and the feet?

If you are examining a chest of drawers ask yourself: how are the drawers constructed on the inside, and what do the handles look like? Do they seem original or are there other, older holes inside the drawers which suggest that the handles might have been replaced? Are there any decorative elements, such as marquetry, carving or gilt-bronze mounts?

As you examine your object, look for signs of physical wear and tear on the feet and the backs of chair legs, on drawer linings and on any moving parts. 'Where you naturally handle or lift your piece of furniture,' suggests dealer and *Antiques Roadshow* furniture expert John Bly, 'check for the sign of other hands that should have done the same thing over the years.' In true 'criminal' style these former users will have left their fingerprints behind: dark, shiny stains under lips, rails and frames, showing how the object has been moved and touched since it was made.

Whatever your piece, give it a good going over! Look behind and underneath it, take drawers out, and check for different types of wood used on the visible and concealed parts of the structure. When photographing the work, it is also a good idea to take close-ups of the more important details of decoration and construction, both for your own researches and to show to experts.

MARKS AND LABELS

Look for a mark or label. Although before the nineteenth century it was very rare for English cabinetmakers to sign their works, French eighteenth-century craftsmen suffered from no such phlegmatic reticence. After 1751, the ébéniste, or cabinetmaker, was obliged by guild regulations to stamp all his works, making life much less difficult for the art detective investigating French furniture from that period.

Nevertheless, it is always worth looking for a name, and you will have to check carefully, because marks are often concealed with a becoming if somewhat irritating modesty. A firm might have identified its furniture with a printed or manuscript label, or with a plate, stamp or stencil.

You might find a signature or initials in ink or pencil, although as Frances Collard, furniture curator at the V&A, warns, in many cases these will be the marks of anonymous outworkers, or perhaps of an upholsterer who subsequently recovered the chair, and as such will not necessarily lead to any positive identification.

Look underneath and behind your piece of furniture. Check the seat rail, the inside legs and the carcases of drawers. Marks can also be hidden under marble tops and behind gilt-bronze mounts; unless you are a furniture restoration expert, do not try to take the tops or mounts off. Remember to look at little details such as casters to see if these have been stamped. Though this might only give you the name of the firm who made the casters, rather than the piece of furniture itself, it can still be useful as an indication of date and quality.

Use your eyes and your common sense and write down a brief description of what you have found. At this stage, it does not matter if you do not have the decorative vocabulary to describe what you find, or that you do not reach any positive conclusions. All you are doing is looking at the object in order to get some idea of how it has been put together and a few points of reference.

II. THE INVESTIGATION

If you have absolutely no idea at all about your piece of furniture and no name or particular information to go on, then the best and the easiest thing to do is to show your photographs and details to a specialist. Go to a museum, an auction house or a good dealer, where you will receive a basic identification, an approximate date, and perhaps even the suggestion of a designer or cabinetmaker. Their assessment will help you to judge whether it is worth taking your research any further. If your furniture is not of any particular interest either academically or in terms of its value, then it is probably not worth proceeding. If, however, you have a name to go on or an intriguing provenance, or if you would simply like to find out more, you can then turn to the libraries.

LIBRARY RESEARCH AND BASIC REFERENCE BOOKS

First, what evidence are you likely to be looking for? Perhaps you want to find another example of your piece of furniture or maybe a design that relates to it. You might want to look up a label, find out more about a certain craftsman, or gather together some information about the former owners of your object and the house whence it came.

A good art history library, preferably one with complete runs of the major art and antiques magazines, will be able to provide you with most of the material you will need to conduct your initial researches (see chapter 3). Publications are legion in this field, so I shall confine myself to suggesting a few basic books and a means of proceeding.

For a general introduction to English furniture, the book that most dealers and experts quote as their bible is *The Dictionary of English Furniture*, revised edition by Ralph Edwards, reprinted by the Antique Collectors' Club in 1983 (paperback edition, 1986). The three-volume dictionary covers its subject from the Middle Ages to the late Georgian period, and is very user-friendly in that, if you turn to 'Bookcases', for example, you will find photographs of a whole selection of bookcases ranging from the seventeenth to the nineteenth centuries, along with a comprehensive text.

Another basic manual that comes highly recommended is Robin Butler's *Arthur Negus Guide to English Furniture* (London, Hamlyn, 1978), which is particularly helpful for information about techniques and construction.

If you have the name of a designer or maker, look them up in the *Dictionary of English Furniture Makers 1660–1840*, edited by G. Beard and C. Gilbert, published by the Furniture History Society in 1986. This is the kind of book that makes the average researcher weak at the knees with admiration and gratitude. Craftsmen are catalogued alphabetically and each entry includes a brief biography, a summary of commissions, a bibliography and a full list of known documentary information and records; it provides a veritable case history for the furniture detective.

Should you be looking for original designs, pattern books by many famous figures, such as Chippendale, Hepplewhite and Sheraton, have been reprinted and are readily available. The Antique Collectors' Club has compiled pictorial dictionaries for eighteenth- and nineteenth-century furniture design, which might also prove helpful.

Whatever the type, nationality or period of the piece of furniture you are researching, comb through the card catalogue and ask the librarian to help you find the volumes best suited to your needs. If you are interested in a specific cabinet-maker, check for any monographs on his work and follow up further leads suggested in the footnotes and bibliography.

You are quite likely to find references to articles in arts magazines. These can offer a wealth of clues to the furniture sleuth, and in many cases will prove to be your major, and perhaps only, source of published information. Art periodicals are useful for their advertisements, as well as for their articles. Major dealers tend to advertise themselves with a classy photograph of one of their more important pieces of furniture, and these can provide a good source for comparison and reference.

In addition to the usual list of magazines (see page 21), there are two seminal journals for anybody seriously interested in the history of furniture: *Furniture History* by the Furniture History Society and *Regional Furniture* by the Regional Furniture Society.

Bibliography

FURNITURE GENERAL

Edwards, Ralph. *Shorter Dictionary of English Furniture*, London, Hamlyn, 1977

Edwards, Ralph and Ramsey, L. G. G. (eds). *The Connoisseur Period Guides*, 6 vols, London, Connoisseur, 1956–61

de Groer, L. *Decorative Arts in Europe 1790–1850*, New York, Rizzoli, 1986

Hayward, Helena (ed). *World Furniture*, London, Hamlyn, 1969

Macquoid, Percy. *A History of English Furniture*, 1904–8, reprinted more recently in both one- and two-volume editions; the Antique Collectors' Club published a two-volume edition in 1987

Payne, Christopher. *19th Century European Furniture*, Woodbridge, Antique Collectors' Club, 1981

Thomas, Dennis (ed). *Connoisseur: The Concise Encyclopaedia of Antiques*, 5 vols, London, National Magazine Co, 1954–61

ENGLISH FURNITURE TO 1700

Cesckinsky, H. and Gribble, E. *Early English Furniture*, London, 1922

Chinnery, Victor. *Oak Furniture: The British Tradition*, Woodbridge, Antique Collectors' Club, 1979

Jervis, Simon. *Printed Furniture Designs Before 1650*, London, Furniture History Society, 1977

Symonds, R. W. *Furniture Making in Seventeenth and*

Eighteenth Century England, London, National Magazine Co, 1955

ENGLISH FURNITURE 1700–1800

Beard, G. *The Work of Robert Adam*, London, John Bartholomew & Son, 1978

Coleridge, W. A. *Chippendale Furniture*, London, Faber & Faber, 1968

Edwards, Ralph and Jourdain, M. *Georgian Cabinet-makers*, London, Country Life, 1955

Fowler, John and Cornforth, John. *English Decoration in the 18th Century,* London, Barrie & Jenkins, 1974

Gilbert, Christopher. *The Life and Works of Thomas Chippendale*, London, Studio Vista Publishers, 1979

Harris, Eileen. *The Furniture of Robert Adam*, London, Alec Tiranti, 1963

Hayward, Helena. *Thomas Johnson and English Rococo*, London, Alec Tiranti, 1964

Musgrave, C. *Adam and Hepplewhite and Other Neo-classical Furniture*, London, Faber & Faber, 1966

Tomlin, M. *Catalogue of Adam Period Furniture*, London, Victoria & Albert Museum, 1972

Ward-Jackson, Peter. *English Furniture Designs of the Eighteenth Century*, London, Victoria & Albert Museum, 1958, reprinted 1984

ENGLISH FURNITURE 1800–1914
General:

Agius, Pauline. *British Furniture, 1880–1915*, Woodbridge, Antique Collectors' Club, 1978

Joy, Edward T. *English Furniture, 1800–51*, London, Sotheby Parke Bernet Publications, 1977

Regency Furniture:

Collard, Frances. *Regency Furniture, 1790–1940*, Woodbridge, Antique Collectors' Club, 1985

Harris, J. *Regency Furniture Designs*, London, Alec Tiranti, 1961

Jourdain, M. *Regency Furniture 1795–1820*, London, Country Life, 1934

VICTORIAN FURNITURE

Allwood, R. *Victorian Furniture*, Woodbridge, Antique Collectors' Club, 1990

Cooper, Jeremy. *Victorian and Edwardian Furniture and Interiors*, London, Thames & Hudson, 1987

Jervis, Simon. *Victorian Furniture*, London, Ward Lock, 1968

Symonds R. W. and Whineray, B. B. *Victorian Furniture*, London, Studio Editions, 1987

Arts and Crafts:

Anscombe, Isabelle and Gere, Charlotte. *The Arts and Crafts Movement in Britain and America*, London, Academy Editions, 1979

Naylor, G. *The Arts and Crafts Movement: A Study of Its Sources, Ideals and Influence on Design Theory*, London, Studio Vista Publishers, 1971

Art Nouveau:

Duncan, Alastair. *Art Nouveau Furniture*, London, Thames & Hudson, 1982

TWENTIETH CENTURY FURNITURE GENERAL

Anscombe, Isabelle and Grey, Howard. *Omega and After*, London, Thames & Hudson, 1985

Battersby, Martin. *The Decorative Twenties*, London, Studio Vista Publishers, 1969

The Decorative Thirties, London, Studio Vista Publishers, 1971

Garner, Philippe. *Contemporary Decorative Arts from 1940 to the Present Day*, Oxford, Phaidon Press, 1980

Twentieth Century Furniture, Oxford, Phaidon Press, 1980

Hillier, Bevis. *Art Deco of the 20s and 30s*, London, Studio Vista Publishers, 1968

Austerity Binge: the Decorative Arts of the 40s and 50s, London, 1972

Lesieutre, A. *Art Deco*, London, 1974

Mang, Karl. *History of Modern Furniture*, Germany, Verlag Gerd Hatje, 1979

Naylor, G. *The Bauhaus*, London, Studio Vista Publishers, 1968

Sparke, Penny. *Furniture*, Twentieth Century Design Series, London, Bell & Hyman, 1986

ENGLISH REGIONAL FURNITURE

Cotton, Bernard D. *English Regional Chairs*, Woodbridge, Antique Collectors' Club, 1990

Gilbert, Christopher. *English Vernacular Furniture 1790–1900*, London, Yale University Press, 1991

FRENCH FURNITURE

Kjellberg, P. *Le Mobilier Français*, 2 vols, Paris, 1978

Ledoux-Lebard, D. *Les Ébénistes Parisiens, 1795–1870*, Paris, 1965
    Les Ébénistes du XIXe Siècle, Paris, 1984

Nicolay, Jean. *L'Art et la Manière des Ébénistes Français au 18ème Siècle*, Paris, 1956–9

de Salverte, Comte François. *Les Ébénistes du XVIIIème Siècle*, Paris, 1934/5 (a useful book in which to look up French stamps)

Verlet, P. *French Furniture and Interior Decoration of the 18th Century*, London, Barrie & Jenkins, 1967

GERMAN FURNITURE

Kreisel, H. *Die Kunst des Deutschen Mobels*, 3 vols, Munich, 1968–70

ITALIAN FURNITURE

Gonzales-Palacios, A. *Il Mobile nei Secoli*, 3 vols, Milan, Italy, 1969

RUSSIAN FURNITURE

Cheneviere, A. *Russian Furniture: The Golden Age, 1780–1840*, London, Weidenfeld & Nicolson, 1988

📖 **FURTHER ENQUIRIES AND SPECIALIST LIBRARIES**

Unfortunately, there is no Witt Library for furniture. Perhaps the closest equivalent is the Photographic Survey of English and European Furniture held by the Furniture and Woodwork Department at the V&A, which is probably the best place to go when beginning any serious furniture investigations.

The Victoria & Albert Museum, London
Furniture and Woodwork Department
Tel: 071 938 8282/8284

The department offers a wide-ranging information service and is a central place for the furniture detective. It is useful both for its own services and material and as a stepping stone to other sources.

Consultations and opinions are given on Tuesday afternoons (2.30–4.30) and subjects covered include: British, European and North American furniture; woodwork from the Renaissance to the present day; leather; treen; upholstery; interior design; and musical instruments. Telephone in advance to ensure that the appropriate curator will be available.

For general research, the department will supply bibliographies on topics ranging from major themes, such as 'English Furniture, 16th–20th Century', to more specific subjects such as 'Church Furnishings' or 'The History of the Bed'. If you approach them with a particular enquiry, say the development of the eighteenth-century chimneypiece, they can also help you form a bibliography from their own card index system, which will refer you to books and articles, original designs, pieces in collections and archives at the V&A and elsewhere.

The departmental library is open to the serious researcher by appointment. One of its great joys is the aforementioned Photographic Survey of English and European Furniture. This is a vast indexed collection of photographs, culled throughout the years from catalogues and magazines, that includes photographs of furniture in public and private collections, many of which are unpublished. Much of the survey is on microfiche. Photographs are catalogued by nationality, object and period; each century is divided into quarters, which makes it very easy to consult.

I once researched an English commode, *circa* 1740, decorated with a particularly unusual ormolu frieze and very fine marquetry. I needed to know if there were any similar pieces extant, so I turned to the English furniture section of the survey, and looked up 'commodes – second quarter of the eighteenth century'. I came across two similar works with identical mounts and closely related decoration. The notes appended to the photographs told me which collections they came from.

Some of the photographs are anonymous, but many will refer you to a sales catalogue, a publication, or a collection, and some will also give you the name of a maker. You can then follow up these clues in subsequent investigations.

If you know the name of the house from which your commode comes, or the commode's maker, you can then consult one of the box-files lining the walls of the department. These can contain anything from a single article clipped from a 1930s issue of *Country Life* to a photocopy of an eighteenth-century household inventory, a doctoral thesis on your crafts-man's work, sale catalogues, and more photographs.

The V&A is a great place for gathering your clues together and for getting good advice, since the curators are both knowledgeable and helpful. They are also, like all museum staff, threatened with cutbacks and are extremely busy, so do not waste their time.

Apart from the libraries mentioned in chapter 3, other London libraries that could also be useful include:

London College of Furniture
41 Commercial Road
London E1
Tel: 071 320 1000
Term time: Mon, Fri: 9–5; Tues–Thurs: 9–7

The London College of Furniture has a comprehensive reference library that is open to the general public in academic term time. The library specialises in the history of furniture, interior decoration and musical instruments. It also holds some archives, including material pertaining to East End cabinet-makers.

Victoria Library (see page 38)

This important local history library holds the records of the leading English furnituremaker Gillows from 1731 to 1932. The material is remarkably comprehensive and includes ledgers, estimate sketchbooks, letter books, etc. If you do not wish to consult the material yourself, the library has their own heritage researcher who will search the records for a fee. The library also holds the archives of the Liberty's firm, and has a large collection of trade directories dating from the late eighteenth century to the present day.

✍ III. EXPERT WITNESSES: MUSEUMS AND MISCELLANEOUS SOURCES

Many museums, galleries and stately homes contain important collections of furniture, and the following list is only a small representative selection. As you proceed with your detective work, you will be able to identify from published sources and word of mouth which collections and curators will be the most helpful to your investigations. Whatever the nature of your individual quest, the Victoria and Albert Museum is probably a good starting point.

🏛 MUSEUMS

London

ARTS AND CRAFTS
William Morris Gallery

This museum deals with the life and works of William Morris and the Arts and Crafts Movement in general. The library is open on request; the archives include material relating to Morris and contemporaries such as Arthur Mackmurdo, founder of the Century Guild. Identifications are made by appointment and by post.

EAST LONDON FURNITURE MAKERS
Geffrye Museum

The main object of the museum is the English domestic interior from 1600 to 1950. There is a collection devoted to the East London furniture trade, and catalogues and archives may be consulted on request. Consultations are available by appointment and by post.

FRENCH FURNITURE
The Wallace Collection

Regional

ARTS AND CRAFTS
Cheltenham Art Gallery and Museum

The museum specialises in furniture and metalwork of the
Arts and Crafts Movement from 1856 until the present day.
The collection is of international importance. The museum
holds a large archive of material concerning Ernest Gimson,
as well as smaller archives on Sidney Barnsley, Harry Davoll,
Norman Jewson, Paul Woodroffe, Fred Griggs, and others.
Consultations are offered by post, or by appointment on
Wednesdays from 2–5.

ART NOUVEAU/DECO
Brighton Museum and Art Gallery

The Brighton Museum specialises in twentieth-century design
generally, including Art Nouveau and Art Deco. Consultations are available on Wednesday afternoons, 2.30–4, by
appointment.

ENGLISH FURNITURE GENERAL
Temple Newsam House, Leeds

The house's superb display of decorative arts focuses on
English works, and the furniture collection is particularly
important. The library is open to the public by prior arrangement; its material includes the archives of the Regional
Furniture Society, and a large collection of Victorian trade
catalogues. Curator Christopher Gilbert is a noted furniture
historian and author of *The Life and Works of Thomas Chippendale* (see page 94), the seminal work on the cabinetmaker.
Consultations are available by appointment.

GILLOWS FURNITURE
Judges' Lodgings, Lancaster

Furniture and archives of the famous Lancastrian cabinet-
makers are housed here.

JAPANNED WARE
Bantock House Museum, Wolverhampton

The museum contains an important collection of eighteenth- and nineteenth-century West Midlands Japanned ware (papier mâché, tin, etc). The museum's archives include the pattern books and trade catalogues of various Japanning factories. Consultations are available by appointment.

TREEN
Birmingham City Museum and Art Gallery

Edward and Eva Pinto devoted a lifetime to collecting an amazing variety of wooden bygones, or treen, dating from the Middle Ages onwards. Their fascinating collection, now housed in Birmingham City Museum, illustrates tools and techniques, and includes objects designed for both domestic and working use. Edward Pinto also compiled the classic book on the subject, *Treen and Other Wooden Bygones* (London, G. Bell & Sons, 1969).

TUNBRIDGE WARE
Tunbridge Wells Museum and Art Gallery

The museum has a large collection of Tunbridge ware, wood-work decorated with parquetry and marquetry, which was a speciality of the area. There is a limited archive on Tunbridge ware manufacturers. The library is open by arrangement; identifications are made by appointment and by post. A seminal book on Tunbridge ware was written by the Pintos: E. H. and E. R. Pinto, *Tunbridge and Scottish Souvenir Woodware* (London, G. Bell & Sons, 1970).

THE WINDSOR CHAIR
Wycombe Local History and Chair Museum,
High Wycombe

High Wycombe has been a centre of the chair-making industry since the eighteenth century. The museum concentrates on the furniture history of the area and specialises in chairs, especially Windsors. The library is open by appointment, and specific enquiries are dealt with by correspondence.

Northern Ireland

IRISH FURNITURE
Ulster Museum, Belfast

Scotland

ART NOUVEAU/DECO AND CHARLES RENNIE MACKINTOSH
Hunterian Art Gallery, Glasgow

✉ **MISCELLANEOUS USEFUL ADDRESSES**

Geological Identification

If you have any kind of stony problem or mineral query, the
Geological Museum (now part of the Natural History
Museum) might well be able to help if you telephone for an
appointment with the appropriate curator. I was once given
the unenviable task of investigating a circular tabletop inlaid
with some 240 specimen marbles and hardstones, most of
them different. With the invaluable assistance of an expert
witness from the Geological Museum, we were able to identify a majority of the stones.

Wood Identification

The Royal Botanic Gardens at Kew (Tel: 081 940 1171) run a
service using microscopic analysis to identify wood. They do
need a small sample of the wood to submit to investigation,
so I would recommend only consulting them when identification is crucial.

✉ **SPECIALIST SOCIETIES**

The Furniture History Society and the Regional Furniture
Society (RFS) are Britain's two major furniture societies.
Their membership includes leading academics, major dealers
and amateur enthusiasts – in other words, lots of very useful
people who could help you with your research and share in
your discoveries. The societies act as great centres of knowledge. As well as a journal, the RFS produces a regular

newsletter, which offers an open forum for members' enquiries and interests, and it has compiled a major and expanding archive of material relating to the furniture-making trades, located at Temple Newsam House in Leeds. Both societies are actively keen to promote new research and can offer invaluable assistance. If your interest in furniture history is more than a passing fancy, they are well worth joining.

Regional Furniture Society
The Membership Secretary
Trouthouse
Warrens Cross
Lechlade
Gloucestershire GL7 3DR
Tel: 0367 52880

The Furniture History Society
c/o The Furniture and Woodwork Department
The Victoria & Albert Museum
London SW7 2RL.

11

Ceramics

Remember to treat your ceramics with care at all times. Be particularly gentle with lids, applied decoration and handles. Ceramics and *Antiques Roadshow* expert David Batty advises never to pick up pots by the handle but always to place your hands round the body or inside. He is speaking from bitter experience, since he recalls one occasion when he inadvertently snapped off the handle of a punter's Minton tureen. 'Have you ever thought about having your piece insured? . . .' Be very careful with cleaning. Wash or wipe the item with lukewarm soapy water, and do not use bleach or any abrasive material.

The difficulty with investigating ceramics is that only knowledge and experience will allow you to distinguish easily between hard and soft paste porcelain or between a fake and a genuine item. Marks were frequently forged and a pair of interlaced 'L's does not necessarily mean that your pot is a piece of Sèvres. French porcelain was faked in England, and Bow and Chelsea were produced in nineteenth-century Paris. A mark should therefore never be relied upon as the sole test of authenticity. If in doubt, consult a specialist.

✍ I. Examine the Evidence

'Use common sense and the experience you will have gathered watching programmes such as the *Antiques Roadshow*,' advises ceramics dealer Mary Wise.

First, you will need to establish if your piece is pottery or porcelain. Hold it up to the light. If it is translucent, it is likely to be porcelain; if not, pottery.

Where does your ceramic come from? Do you think it is Eastern or Western?

Look at the overall design and turn the piece over to see if there is a mark. According to the Ceramics Department at the V&A, an astonishing number of people come in without having looked at their ceramics properly. Either photograph or transcribe the mark, remembering to include any odd numbers, dots or squiggly bits that appear on the back, since these could well be pattern references that might enable you to identify the piece in a relevant publication.

It does not necessarily matter if there is no mark since, depending on what your object is, this need not affect either its interest or its value. Indeed as Jonathan Horne, leading dealer and expert in early English pottery, remarks, 'Most pieces in my field aren't marked before the nineteenth century, and if I find a mark, I am a bit suspicious.'

Examine the ceramic in detail. If you think it is porcelain, is it soft or hard paste? Only experience or an expert will be able to confirm this for sure, but as a rough guide and as their descriptions suggest 'hard paste' has a hard, bright, glassy look, while 'soft paste' is softer and creamier.

What is the surface of the ceramic like? Is there any moulded decoration? Is it printed or painted, and are the designs over or underneath the glaze? Look closely at the piece and run your fingernail gently over the surface to feel for different textures.

Do not worry if you cannot answer these questions. 'Technical details don't really matter too much at this stage,' advises ceramics dealer Deborah Gage. 'Nationality is by far the most important thing to establish so that you can look up the piece in the right book or show it to the relevant expert.'

So, in brief, look at the piece carefully and write as full a description of it as you can, including the measurements (height and diameter). Photograph the object, transcribe or photograph the marks, and note down any provenance details. Refer to Part One for general information about conducting your investigation.

A Few Tips About Marks

If the country of origin appears after the mark, your piece will almost certainly have been made after 1891; the phrase 'Made in England' denotes a twentieth-century date. The use of the words 'Limited' or 'Ltd', 'Trade Mark', and 'Royal' all indicate that the piece post-dates the middle of the nineteenth century, and the term 'Established' suggests a date after about 1875.

A diamond-shaped registration mark was used on Victorian ceramics from 1842 to 1883 (see page 55); thereafter it was superseded by the appearance of 'RD No' followed by numerals. If the number exceeds 360,000, then the date of registration is after 1900.

Any printed mark incorporating the Royal Arms is nineteenth century or later. A mark including the name of the pattern may be regarded as later than 1810. Finally, the description 'Bone China' or 'English Bone China' indicates a twentieth-century date.

✍ II. THE INVESTIGATION

If the piece is not marked and you have no idea what it is, go straight to a specialist (see page 111). If, however, you have a name or a mark, it is worth a quick preliminary visit to the local art reference library, where you will be able to look up the mark, dig out the relevant books and identify the best place to go for further advice.

📖 LIBRARY RESEARCH AND BASIC REFERENCE BOOKS

There are innumerable books on pottery and porcelain. As more research is carried out on individual types and factories, so new volumes appear, many reproducing archives, pattern books and much of the material you are likely to need. General guides, such as those listed below, offer a good introduction to the subject, providing help with identification, dating, interpreting marks, and so on. Illustrated books are also useful since they allow you to contrast and compare your piece with originals, although, as Continental ceramics dealer Armin B. Allen warns, beware: just because you find the illustration of a Meissen harlequin figure, *circa* 1740, which looks identical to yours, this does not mean that your piece is of the same date. It could be a later reproduction from the same model.

If you already know the name of your factory – Derby for example – look it up in the library card index and consult the relevant books. The bibliographies will refer you to further sources. Also, the ceramics departments at certain museums, such as the V&A and Stoke-on-Trent City Museum, will supply bibliographies relating to general themes and to specific factories.

Although it is sensible to use the most recent books, which will contain the most up-to-date research, do not reject a book just because it has an early publication date. Many classic works, particularly on Continental porcelain, were compiled in the early 1900s and remain invaluable sources of reference, if only for their pictures.

Bibliography

MARKS
Generally acknowledged as the best book for English marks is Geoffrey A. Godden's *Encyclopaedia of British Pottery and Porcelain Marks* (London, Barrie & Jenkins, 1979). As David Batty notes, this is the bible for English ceramic collectors, so much so that the author's name is abbreviated in the trade to 'God'.

Chaffers, William B. *Marks and Monograms on European and Oriental Pottery and Porcelain*, London, William Reeves Booksellers, 1975
Cushion, John P. and Honey, William Bowyer. *Handbook of Pottery and Porcelain Marks*, 4th rev ed, London, Faber & Faber, 1980

Danckert, Ludwig. *Directory of European Porcelain: Marks, Makers and Factories*, London, N.A.G. Press, 1981

Davison, Gerald. *A Guide to Marks on Chinese Porcelain*, London, Bamboo Publishing, 1987

ENGLISH POTTERY AND PORCELAIN GENERAL

Berthoud, Michael. *An Anthology of British Cups*, Wingham, Micawber Publications, 1982

Bradshaw, Peter. *18th Century English Porcelain Figures*, Woodbridge, Antique Collectors' Club, 1981

Cameron, Elisabeth (ed). *Encyclopaedia of Pottery and Porcelain: Nineteenth and Twentieth Centuries*, London, Faber & Faber, 1986

Charleston, Robert J. *English Porcelain, 1745–1850*, London, Ernest Benn, 1965
and Towner, Donald C. *English Ceramics, 1580–1830*, London, Sotheby Parke Bernet Publications, 1977

Garner, F. H. and Archer, Michael. *English Delftware*, London, Faber & Faber, 1972

Godden, Geoffrey A. *British Porcelain: An Illustrated Guide*, London, Barrie & Jenkins, 1974
British Pottery: An Illustrated Guide, London, Barrie & Jenkins, 1974
Eighteenth Century English Porcelain, London, Grafton Books, 1985
Encyclopaedia of British Porcelain Manufacturers, London, Barrie & Jenkins, 1988
Godden's Guide to English Porcelain, London, Granada Publishing, 1978
Illustrated Encyclopaedia of British Pottery and Porcelain, London, Barrie & Jenkins, 1966
Victorian Porcelain, London, Barrie & Jenkins, 1961

Horne, Jonathan. *English Tin Glazed Tiles*, London, J. Horne, 1989

Jewitt, L. *The Ceramic Art of Great Britain* (1878) rev ed, London, Barrie & Jenkins, 1972

Lane, Arthur. *English Porcelain Figures of the Eighteenth Century*, London, Faber & Faber, 1961

Miller, Phillip and Berthoud, Michael. *An Anthology of British Teapots*, Wingham, Micawber Publications, 1985

Sandon, Henry. *British Pottery and Porcelain for Pleasure and Investment*, London, John Gifford, 1969

Watney, Dr Bernard. *English Blue and White Porcelain of the 18th Century*, rev ed, London, Faber & Faber, 1971

Wills, Geoffrey. *English Pottery and Porcelain*, London, Guinness Superlatives, 1969

CONTINENTAL CERAMICS

Brunet, M. and Preaud, T. *Sèvres, Des Origines à nos Jours*, Fribourg, 1978

Charleston, Robert J. (ed). *World Ceramics: An Illustrated History*, London, Hamlyn Publishing Group, 1981

Eriksen, Svend and de Bellaigue, Geoffrey. *Sèvres Porcelain: Vincennes and Sèvres, 1740–1800*, London, Faber & Faber, 1987

Hayward, J. F. *Viennese Porcelain of the Du Paquier Period*, London, Rockliff Publishing Corporation, 1952

Honey, William Bowyer. *German Porcelain*, London, Faber & Faber, 1947

Dresden China, London, Faber & Faber, 1954

de Jonge, C. H. *Delft Ceramics*, New York, 1970

Meister, Peter Wilhelm and Reber, Horst. *European Porcelain of the Eighteenth Century*, Oxford, Phaidon Press, 1983

Pauls-Eisenbeiss, E. *German Porcelain of the 18th Century*, Fribourg, 1972

Savage, George. *17th and 18th Century French Porcelain*, London, Barrie & Rockliff, 1960

Verlet, Pierre. *Sèvres*, Paris, 1953

Ware, George W. *German and Austrian Porcelain*, Frankfurt, nd

Wynter, Harriet. *An Introduction to European Porcelain*, New York, 1972

★

THE PRINCIPAL CATEGORIES OF PORCELAIN

1. Hard Paste

CHINESE: T'ang Dynasty onwards.

MEISSEN: 1710 onwards and virtually all German factories.

ITALIAN: some factories, especially Vezzi Venice and
  Doccia.

FRENCH: most factories went over to hard paste in the
  decade or two after the discovery of Kaolin near
  Limoges in 1768.

ENGLISH: Bristol. An abortive factory was started in
  1765, following William Cookworthy's recogni-
  tion of china clay and stone in Cornwall. Serious
  production began in Plymouth in 1768 and trans-
  ferred to Bristol in 1770; the patent was sold to
  Staffordshire, hence New Hall (see below).

2. Hard Paste with Soft Glaze

ENGLISH: New Hall (Staffordshire), Caughley-Coalport
  and perhaps others.

USA: some modern American porcelain.

3. Soft Paste

ITALIAN: Florence (Medici Porcelain 1575–1587), Capo-
  dimonte (Naples 1743–1759).

FRENCH: all factories were in Rouen from the late seventeenth century until 1768, with the exception of
  Strasbourg and other north-eastern French factories relying on German influence and skill. Sèvres
  continued to produce both hard and soft paste for
  some years after 1768.

ENGLISH: all eighteenth-century factories produced soft
  paste, except Plymouth, Cookworthy's Bristol,
  and New Hall. After 1800 most factories went
  over to bone china.

4. Bone China

ENGLAND: from the nineteenth century onwards this has
  been the standard porcelain body for the British
  Isles. With a few exceptions, very little bone
  china has been produced elsewhere.

(compiled by the Ceramics Department at the V&A)

★

✍ III. EXPERT WITNESSES: MUSEUMS AND MISCELLANEOUS SOURCES

There are many fine collections of ceramics in Britain, a number of which specialise in the works of a particular factory. Remember, if you are investigating works from a specific geographical area, it is often worth consulting the relevant local museum and county record office for further information. Many interesting discoveries in the field of British ceramics have also been made by archaeological societies, whose journals and meetings can provide helpful clues.

If the factory that made your piece is still in business, contact them as they might well have a museum or an archivist who can help with your enquiries (see below for examples). If records have been well preserved, it is possible you might come up with some fascinating material.

I once investigated a highly important Sèvres vase. A letter to the Sèvres factory and museum in France uncovered not only the original designs and details of all the artists and craftsmen who had worked on it, but also revealed that the vase had been presented, as a diplomatic sweetener, by Talleyrand to Viscount Castlereagh at the Congress of Vienna in 1814, when the greatest Ambassadors of Europe met in the wake of the Napoleonic Wars. Suddenly the vase was no longer just a flashily decorated and oversized porcelain pot, but a piece of political history, and an example of research at its most glorious and satisfying best.

Finally, do not forget to consult the dealers, since many are undoubtedly the leading experts in their field, and in my experience are extremely generous with information. Contact BADA and LAPADA. To see a pick of the best, you can always visit the International Ceramics Fair, held every June at the Dorchester Hotel in London.

🏛 MUSEUMS

For general ceramics advice, the two best museums to consult are probably the V&A and Stoke-on-Trent City Museum.

The Victoria & Albert Museum, London
Ceramics Department

The V&A houses a magnificent collection of ceramics and, in common with all other departments, the Ceramics Department offers an opinion and enquiries service on Tuesday afternoons, 2.30–4.30. The department deals with all Western ceramics. For Chinese, Japanese and Oriental works you should consult the Far Eastern Department, and for Indian pieces, the Indian Department (same times). The advantage of the V&A is that the scope of both its collection and expertise is international, and the Ceramics Department estimate that roughly fifty per cent of the works brought in are Continental. In addition to examining works, the department also supplies bibliographies.

Stoke-on-Trent City Museum and Art Gallery

Located in the heart of the Potteries, the museum holds one of the finest collections of pottery and porcelain in the world. The museum follows the history of Stoke-on-Trent as the centre of English ceramic production. There is an outstanding collection of Staffordshire ware and major examples of work from factories including Wedgwood, Longton Hall, New Hall, Spode, Davenport, Ridgway and other local factories. Nineteenth-century art pottery and work by twentieth-century ceramicists are also well represented. Opinions are given on Wednesdays, 2–4.30. The public library at Stoke-on-Trent has also formed a collection relating specifically to ceramics.

Other museums with good general collections of ceramics include:

Brighton Museum and Art Gallery

The museum is the home of the Willet Collection of English pottery from the seventeenth to the nineteenth centuries.

Fitzwilliam Museum, Cambridge

The Fitzwilliam has a good collection of Eastern and Western pottery and porcelain, and the finest collection of

Korean ceramics in the West. Consultations are available by appointment.

Manchester City Art Gallery

The museum houses a major collection of English earthenware and a fine selection of eighteenth-century work from English and European factories.

Museums and collections specialising in the works of individual potteries and from specific areas include:

BELLEEK PORCELAIN AND CERAMICS GENERAL
National Museum of Ireland, Dublin

COALPORT CHINA AND DECORATIVE TILES
Ironbridge Gorge Museum Trust, Telford

This industrial museum is composed of six main museum sites, including: the Coalport China Works, housing a magnificent display of Coalport china; the Jackfield Works and Tile Museum, with a collection of decorative tiles by such firms as Craven Dunhill and Maw & Co; and the Coalbrookdale Museum of Iron. The library is open by appointment, and holds archives and catalogues relating to firms whose work is exhibited, as well as material connected with the art of the Industrial Revolution. Enquiries are answered by appointment and by post.

DERBY PORCELAIN
City of Derby Museums and Art Gallery

The museum specialises in objects relating to Derby, including a Derby porcelain collection of international importance. The archive material held by the museum includes watercolours by Derby porcelain decorators. Identifications are made by appointment and by post.

Royal Crown Derby Museum
Royal Crown Derby Porcelain Co Ltd, Derby

This private museum specialises in the history of Derby Porcelain from 1750 to the present day. The firm's archives, though restricted, can be consulted by appointment. There is an open day for consultations on the first Tuesday of every month, but specialist staff are available every day.

DEVON POTTERY
Royal Albert Memorial Museum, Exeter

North and South Devon pottery are the focus of the collection, and archives relate to Devon potters. Identifications are made by appointment.

LIVERPOOL CERAMICS AND CERAMICS GENERAL
Liverpool Museum

The ceramics collection extends from the Middle Ages to the present day, and includes both British and European works. It is especially strong in Liverpool ceramics (Delftware, porcelain and the Herculaneum factory), Wedgwood wares, and twentieth-century studio pottery. Oriental ceramics are curated by the Antiquities Department. The museum holds a number of archives relating to Liverpool's ceramics industry, in particular to John Sadler and the Herculaneum Pottery. Other relevant archives are kept at the Liverpool Record Office at Liverpool Central Library, which is adjacent to the museum. Consultations are available by appointment, and items can be left at the museum for assessment. The museum has opened a Ceramic Study Centre, giving access to the reserve collection, documentation, reference books, etc. Phone for an appointment and for further information.

Williamson Art Gallery and Museum, Birkenhead

The museum houses an important collection of Liverpool porcelain. Consultations are available by appointment and by post.

LOWESTOFT PORCELAIN
Norwich Castle Museum

The museum has the finest public collection of Lowestoft porcelain in the world. It also houses a collection of British ceramic teapots, 1700–1860.

MARTINWARE POTTERY
Pitshanger Manor Museum, London

The museum has a good display of Martinware pottery and also curates the collection of Martinware at Southall Library. The library is open by appointment, and the material there includes copies of documents and published material on the Martin brothers. Consultations are available by appointment.

MINTON
The Minton Museum, Stoke-on-Trent

The museum covers the history of Minton wares from 1793 until the present day, and holds a remarkably comprehensive archive of pattern books and records. Consultations are available by appointment.

ROCKINGHAM
Rotherham Art Gallery

The Rotherham Museum and Gallery holds a major collection of Rockingham porcelain, and examples of local pottery and glass. It has some archival material. Consultations are available by appointment.

ROYAL DOULTON
Sir Henry Doulton Gallery
Royal Doulton Ltd, Stoke-on-Trent

The gallery has examples of Royal Doulton spanning over 170 years, and includes the Royal Doulton Figure Collection. Some archival material has been preserved. Consultations are available by appointment.

SPODE
Spode Museum, Stoke-on-Trent

The museum specialises in the products of the Spode manufactory, transfer printing, blue and white wares, bone china, stone china, Parian and earthenware of the Spode (1770–1833), Copeland (1833–1970) and present-day periods. The majority of Spode Company records are held by the University of Keele, Newcastle-under-Lyme, but some material is still preserved at the factory itself. All enquiries are dealt with by the museum's historical consultant, and consultations are available by appointment.

SUNDERLAND POTTERY
Sunderland Museum and Art Gallery

The museum specialises in local ceramics; archives relate to local glass and pottery manufacturers, including Scott's South-wick Pottery. Consultations are available by appointment.

WEDGWOOD
Wedgwood Museum, Stoke-on-Trent

The museum's focus is on the history of Wedgwood, and it holds a remarkable series of archives connected with the firm. The library is open by appointment, and items can be brought in daily for consultations with staff, although it is always better to ring beforehand. A reader's ticket is necessary if you wish to consult the archives.

WORCESTER PORCELAIN
Dyson Perrins Museum Trust, Worcester

The museum covers the history of Worcester porcelain from 1751 to the present day. The records of the firm can be consulted, and objects can be brought in for identification, by appointment.

WELSH CHINA FACTORIES
Glynn Vivian Art Gallery and Museum, Swansea
National Museum of Wales, Cardiff

YORKSHIRE POTTERIES
Doncaster Museum and Art Gallery

The museum has good collections of English glassware and ceramics, with a particular concentration on the works of the Yorkshire potters; it has some archival material. Consultations are available by appointment.

Yorkshire Museum, York

A strong collection of Yorkshire pottery is on display and a good departmental library can be made available to serious enquirers. Consultations are available by appointment.

CONTINENTAL CERAMICS
Sèvres

Sèvres porcelain is unique, not only in terms of its quality, but also by virtue of the fact that many of the factory's records have been preserved. Their wonderful eighteenth-century ledgers provide a fascinating insight into daily life at

Versailles. I once researched a short history of snuff and tobacco. The Sèvres sales records showed tobacco jars purchased by Mme de Pompadour, snuff spoons sold to the royal princesses, and elegant floral spittoons dispensed to the ladies and gentlemen of the court. The records can tell you who bought an object, and how much was paid for it. The archives contain details about painters, modellers and the general manufacture of porcelain at the royal factory.

For information about the Sèvres records write to the archivist:

Manufacture Nationale de Sèvres
4 Grande Rue
92310 Sèvres
France

or contact:

The Musée National de Céramique
Place de la Manufacture
92310 Sèvres
France
Tel: 1 45 34 99 05

Closer to hand, the Wallace Collection in London houses a magnificent collection of Sèvres. The library holds on microfiche the records of the Sèvres Factory, which can be consulted by serious researchers, by appointment.

✉ **CERAMIC SOCIETIES**

There are many different ceramic societies which not only provide the opportunity to meet fellow collectors, but can also be of great help to the art detective. Some publish journals, which are a valuable outlet for new research, and most produce some form of newsletter which can be useful for enquiries. Among the most prestigious general societies are the English Ceramic Circle, the Northern Ceramic Society and the Oriental Ceramic Society. There are societies for specific factories – the Wedgwood Society, the Spode Society – as well as for different types and styles of pottery – Friends of Blue, the Pot Lid Circle, the Tiles and Architectural Ceramics Society and so on.

For current details and addresses try contacting the Ceramics Departments at the Victoria & Albert Museum and Stoke-on-Trent City Museum. If you are interested in works of a particular type or factory, the museum – or a dealer – specialising in that area, should be able to put you in contact with the relevant organisation. Useful addresses can also be gleaned from specialist journals.

12

Glass

Investigating glass is no easy matter. Unlike porcelain or silver, most pieces of old glass bear no identifying marks or signatures, and there are comparatively few records or pattern books extant. Though books provide helpful guidelines for identification and dating, perhaps the quickest and safest course of action for the embryonic glass detective is to seek specialist advice.

As with everything else, the best way of truly learning about glass is by handling it and looking at it. Glass dealer Jeanette Hayhurst recommends visiting museums, glass auctions, recognised dealers and antiques fairs. At her gallery in Kensington Church Street, London, she keeps a permanent display of fakes so that customers can see and feel the difference between these and true eighteenth-century pieces. 'There are very few real fakes in glass,' she explains, 'but plenty of reproductions – made at the turn of the nineteenth century, en suite with repro-Georgian furniture. It is these that the new collector should be wary of.'

According to dealer and specialist Andrew Burne, one of the most popular and general misconceptions held about glass is that all good Georgian pieces must be Waterford; another is that Waterford is always blue. Both of these assumptions belong to the realm of mythology rather than art history, and should be avoided.

✍ I. Examine the Evidence

Unless you already have some knowledge of glassmaking procedures and materials, there is no point trying to be too technical at this stage. Just submit your piece to a basic and commonsense examination: look over it carefully, write down what it is, measure the height and diameter, take photographs, and transcribe any known provenance.

In order to help you to scrutinise the evidence more closely, the following clues have been suggested by leading experts. Use their points as a basic guideline, but do not worry if you cannot reach any positive conclusions: that is what you go to a specialist for.

The first thing to establish is whether the glass is blown as opposed to moulded. 'Look for slight irregularities of shape, bubbles, swirls, toolmarks and imperfections,' advises Andrew Burne. 'Check for movement in the glass and a suggestion of the material being in its liquid state.'

What kind of glass is it? Lead crystal should feel heavy in the hand and emit a ring like a dinner-bell when tapped with the fingernail; soda glass, however, is far lighter and less resonant.

Look carefully at the colour: old glass tends to be darker and more varied in tones than its modern equivalent.

Most eighteenth-century tableware has a pontil mark in the centre of the base, where the 'pontil' − the rod used to remove the glass from the blowpipe − has been broken off, leaving a rough patch. If this has been ground off, there may be a polished circle: feel for it with your finger. Though many old glass objects show a pontil mark, so do many fakes, and its presence does not guarantee age.

Look at the overall design of the object. With drinking glasses take particular note of the shape of the bowl and, above all, the stem − the main criterion for dating eighteenth-century English drinking glasses. Examine the foot of a glass both for its form and size. On early glasses, the foot tends to be wider than the rim and, generally speaking, far more generous than its modern equivalents.

Look at the decoration − cutting, engraving, enamelling − and take note of shapes and patterns, which will help you to date the glass. Use your eyes; and use your fingers to test the sharpness and quality of the cutting. Engravings can yield much information and can display events, personalities, and dates. However, it is important to remember that a piece of old glass could have been engraved at any later period, and that the work itself could have been produced long after the occasion it celebrates.

Refer to Part One for more general information about conducting your investigation.

✍ II. THE INVESTIGATION

📖 LIBRARY RESEARCH AND BASIC REFERENCE BOOKS

At the library you will be able to compare and contrast your piece with other examples reproduced in books, where you will also find the correct vitreous vocabulary used to describe and classify it. Many volumes include a guide, in the form of line drawings, to shapes and designs throughout the ages, in particular of bowls, stems, knops – the rounded bulge in the stem of a glass – and feet. These are very useful for getting a quick if basic grasp of styles and dates.

Some archives have been preserved in Britain (see museums section for details). A useful source for eighteenth-century designs, notes Jeanette Hayhurst, can be period trade cards; the illustrations on them can help you to trace and compare shapes. Among the most famous of the glass records is the eighteenth-century pattern book of the Nostetangen glass factory in Norway. Published by Ada Polak in *Gammelt Norsk Glass* (Oslo, 1953 – with an English summary), the pattern book provides a unique picture of period shapes and a useful comparison with contemporary English glassware.

Bibliography

Arwas, Victor. *Glass: Art Nouveau to Art Deco*, London, Academy Editions, 1978

Barrington Haynes, E. *Glass Through the Ages*, 1948, revised 1959, London, Penguin, 1969

Bickerton, L. M. *Eighteenth Century English Drinking Glasses:*

An Illustrated Guide, Woodbridge, Antique Collectors'
Club, 1986 (contains a very useful bibliography)

Brooks, John. *The Arthur Negus Guide to British Glass*, London,
Hamlyn Publishing Group, 1981

Charleston, Robert J. *English Glass and the Glass Used in
England Circa 400–1940*, London, Allen & Unwin, 1984
An Illustrated Dictionary of Glass, London, Thames &
Hudson, 1977

Davis, Derek Cecil. *English Bottles and Decanters 1650–1900*,
London, Charles Letts & Co, 1972

Hughes, G. Bernard. *English Glass for the Collector 1660–1860*,
Guildford, Lutterworth Press, 1967

Morris, Barbara. *Victorian Table Glass and Ornaments*, London,
Barrie & Jenkins, 1979

Thorpe, W. A. *A History of English and Irish Glass*, London,
A. & C. Black, 1961

Wakefield, Hugh. *Nineteenth Century British Glass*, 2nd rev
ed, London, Faber & Faber, 1982

✍ III. EXPERT WITNESSES: MUSEUMS AND MISCELLANEOUS SOURCES

Many museums and institutions house collections of glass.
Listed below, I have included specialist glass museums and an
abbreviated selection of general museums with good collections of glass and archives.

In this field, as in all the decorative arts, if you are researching a piece of glass from a specific area or factory, contact the
relevant local history library and museum to see if any work
has been carried out in your particular subject. Many local
museums will also have a good display of glass from archaeological excavations. Do not forget that good dealers and
auction houses can be helpful sources of advice.

🏛 SPECIALIST GLASS MUSEUMS
Broadfield House Glass Museum, Kingswinford

The museum is perhaps the most important centre for glass in the country. It contains examples from the Roman period to the present day, but the collection is richest in the locally produced coloured glass and crystal which made the name of Stourbridge Glass internationally famous in the nineteenth century. Library facilities are provided, and there is a fine collection of records, which include archives of local firms, Thomas Webb's pattern books and, on microfiche, the catalogues of the Corning Glass Museum in the United States. Consultations are available by appointment or by post. The museum provides an information service on all aspects of glass, and if they cannot answer your enquiry themselves, they will endeavour to pass it on to someone who can.

Pilkington Glass Museum, St Helens

This museum specialises in glass in all its forms and holds a collection of both contemporary and antique glass. There is a library that is open to the public by appointment and, although there are no consultation days, individual objects may be brought in and left at the museum for a report. The museum is part of Pilkington plc, and the glass factory's archives are held by the company records department.

Royal Brierly Crystal, Brierly Hill, West Midlands

Still active today, this glass factory dates back to 1824. For most of its history the firm was known as Stevens and Williams. The present company preserves the historical archives and also runs a library and museum containing a collection of seventeenth- to nineteenth-century glass, which includes its own products. Enquiries can be made by appointment or by post, but there is a charge for archival research undertaken by the staff.

The Stained Glass Museum, Ely

The museum specialises in stained glass from the Middle Ages to the present day. There is a library open to the public, and a study collection of glass by different designers and factories that can be viewed by appointment. Postal enquiries are welcomed. The curator adds a specific piece of practical advice for those interested in the study of stained glass: 'Always take binoculars to churches and cathedrals!'

The most famous glass museum in the world, and a major centre for glass research is:

The Corning Museum of Glass
1 Museum Way
Corning, New York 14830
USA
Tel: 0101 607 937 5371

🏛 **MUSEUMS GENERAL**

London

ANTIQUE AND MEDIEVAL GLASS
The British Museum

The British Museum houses one of the world's most outstanding collections of glass. Consultations are available with the relevant department.

GLASS GENERAL
The Victoria & Albert Museum

With its major collection of glass, the V&A is a good place to begin your enquiries. Consultations are available at the Glass and Ceramics Department on Tuesday afternoons.

Regional

GLASS GENERAL
Ashmolean Museum, Oxford

The museum's collection of glass includes Roman glass and seventeenth- and eighteenth-century vessels; its particular strengths are Jacobites and the engraved, stippled and enamelled drinking glasses of the eighteenth century.

Manchester City Art Gallery

This museum houses an important collection of eighteenth-century glass.

GLASS GENERAL, COLOURED GLASS AND CHINESE GLASS
City of Bristol Museum and Art Gallery

Bristol City Art Gallery's collection of glass includes an

important display of coloured glass and the largest collection of Chinese glass in Britain. Consultations are available by appointment.

GLASS GENERAL AND STAINED GLASS
Birmingham City Museum and Art Gallery

Birmingham has a fine glass collection, which includes Venetian glass, lead crystal and a particularly good display of stained glass, with windows designed by Burne-Jones and Rossetti, and works by local manufacturers. A strong archival collection of designs covers both the nineteenth and twentieth centuries.

NORTH-EAST GLASS
Laing Art Gallery, Newcastle-upon-Tyne

The glass section of the collection includes eighteenth-century enamelled glass by William Beilby of Newcastle, and the museum holds the pattern books of North-East pressed glass firms such as Sowerbys. Consultations are available by appointment and by post.

SUNDERLAND GLASS
Sunderland Museum

Northern Ireland

IRISH GLASS AND GLASS GENERAL
Ulster Museum, Belfast

Republic of Ireland

IRISH GLASS AND GLASS GENERAL
National Museum of Ireland, Dublin

Scotland

SCOTTISH GLASS AND GLASS GENERAL
Glasgow Art Gallery and Museum

The Glasgow Art Gallery contains a collection of Scottish, English and Continental glass.

Royal Museum of Scotland, Edinburgh

The museum houses important European, Oriental and

antique glass collections. The library is open by appointment, and consultations are available by prior arrangement.

Wales

GLASS GENERAL AND PAPERWEIGHTS
Glynn Vivian Art Gallery and Museum, Swansea

The glass collection includes fine displays of paperweights and eighteenth- and nineteenth-century glassware.

13
Silver

✍ I. Examine the Evidence

Examine the object, measure it, weigh it on your kitchen scales, photograph it and collect together the provenance details. Transcribe the mark. Aspreys' silver specialist, Charles Truman, recommends either rubbing the mark with a burnt match or blackening it with a candle. Cover the patch with a piece of sellotape and press down firmly. Remove the tape, which should bear the carbon mark, and stick it to a piece of white paper. Obviously, the hallmark is a major clue, although it will not tell the amateur sleuth about the aesthetic quality of an object or whether the piece and the mark itself are genuine.

Hallmarking was first instituted in Britain in 1300. Most British silver, with certain exceptions, will be marked, thus allowing the art detective to identify the place of assay, the standard of the silver, the date of production, and the name, or at least the initials, of the maker. Below I have included a very basic introduction to the system of hallmarking. For further information, refer to the bibliography or consult the Assay Offices (see below).

On British silver there are usually four marks:

1. The 'Hall' or 'Town' Mark, the stamp of the official Assay Office, where the quality of the metal is tested. Today there are four British Assay Offices in London, Birmingham, Sheffield and Edinburgh, although in former times several of the larger provincial cities had an office. Each one has its own symbol, and this is the first mark you should look up in order to be able to decode the date letter.

2. The 'Standard' or Quality Mark, indicates the standard of the silver. Sterling silver bears the lion passant, and Britannia silver, higher in quality, the device of Britannia. Between 1697 and 1715, the lion passant was replaced by a lion's head in profile.

3. The Annual Date Letter shows the year in which the object was hallmarked. Each Assay Office uses different letters to indicate the year; for identification purposes, the shape of the shield containing the letter is almost as important as the letter itself.

4. The Maker or Sponsor's Mark, consists of the initials – or in early times, the symbol – of the maker, manufacturer or retailer who sponsored the article when it was sent for assay. Between 1696 and 1720 the first two letters of the surname were used. Where two or more sponsors have the same initials, there is a variation in the surrounding shield or the style of the letters.

Other marks to be found in addition to these include:

The Sovereign's Head: the mark for the duty which had to be paid on silver and gold items between 1784 and 1890.

The Jubilee Mark: to commemorate George V's Silver Jubilee on items assayed between 1933 and 1936.

The Leopard's Head: London's hallmark, also sometimes used as an additional mark by provincial offices, with the exceptions of Birmingham and Sheffield.

The Coronation Mark: a voluntary mark to celebrate the coronation of Elizabeth II, and applied between 1952 and 1954.

Foreign Silver: from 1843, imported foreign silver articles of the required standard were marked with the letter 'F'.

Generally speaking, on silver from countries other than Britain, the process of marking tends to be less systematised and more irregular. For identifications of foreign marks, see the bibliography.

If you are dealing with a set of items, for example, cutlery or a toilet set, do not just look at one piece and assume that all the other marks will be the same. Even though they appear identical, individual pieces could have been made at different times by different makers to replace damaged works or simply to increase the group, so examine each object separately.

Write down what you think the object is, look at the style and shape, and examine the decoration. Is the piece plain or is it pierced? Is the decoration engraved or in relief? Are patterns purely decorative, or do they represent some form of narrative scene? Is there an inscription, an armorial, or any symbols that might be of some significance?

Take note of whatever you find, yet maintain the detective's customary cynicism. Silver has always lent itself to reworking. An originally plain eighteenth-century tankard could have been lavishly decorated in the nineteenth century, armorials could have been added later, or conversely removed at some stage during the history of the piece. While the amateur sleuth cannot be expected to recognise such alterations, it is something to be aware of (also see page 130).

Following on from this, if you want to preserve the value of your antique silver item, do not have it engraved with a loving message or indeed anything else. Silver collectors are purists, and any later engraving, be it ever so romantic or witty, will undoubtedly reduce its worth.

Also, be careful with cleaning. Dealer Michael Bell, from the Bond Street silver shop S. J. Phillips, told me sadly how, in his opinion, much silver had been irretrievably damaged by the over-zealous polishing of English butlers and gentlemen's gentlemen in the 1920s and '30s, thus wearing away the silver, and rendering hallmarks illegible.

Today's poor substitute for a Jeeves, the dishwasher, can be equally harmful. So, to clean silver, wash it in hot soapy water, dry it carefully with a soft cloth, and polish it with a soft cloth or a chamois leather. Never use abrasive polishes to remove the tarnish, and be particularly careful when cleaning hallmarks, since it is important that they should be as sharp as possible. Always empty salt cellars, as salt corrodes silver, and store all silver in acid-free tissue paper.

Refer to Part One for more general information about conducting your investigation.

DETECTIVE BEWARE

According to silver expert and Christie's deputy chairman James Collingridge, marks added to silver plate in the nineteenth century to simulate genuine silver hallmarks are perhaps the most common cause of confusion among those bringing their objects in to be valued. There are also a number of circumstances in which articles made post-1300 are actually illegal according to the Hallmarking Act of 1973. These include unauthorised alterations of usage – for example, mugs turned into jugs – unhallmarked repairs, faked hallmarks and transposed hallmarks, when a mark taken from a small item would be added to a larger work in order to avoid paying full excise duty. To the layman, the laws governing silver are of such bewildering complexity that they might have been compiled by the writers of 'Yes, Minister'. For an account of current regulations, arm yourself with a copy of the 1973 Hallmarking Act; for an explanation of these 'illegal' works, see the article 'Old Silver and the Law' published in the *Antique Collector*, April 1989. When in doubt, contact the Assay Office.

✍ II. THE INVESTIGATION

📖 LIBRARY RESEARCH AND BASIC REFERENCE BOOKS

If you want to try looking up the marks yourself, there are any number of publications on silver, but the basic bibles for British marks and makers include:

Bradbury, Frederick. *Book of Hall Marks*, Sheffield, J. W. Northend, 1989

Culme, John. *The Directory of London Gold & Silversmiths and Allied Traders 1838–1914*, Woodbridge, Antique Collectors' Club, 1987

Grimwade, A. *London Goldsmiths, 1697–1837: Their Marks and Lives from the Original Registers at Goldsmiths' Hall and Other Sources*, 3rd rev ed, London, Faber & Faber, 1990

Pickford, Ian (ed). *Jackson's Silver and Gold Marks of England, Scotland and Ireland*, Woodbridge, Antique Collectors' Club, 1989

For foreign marks consult:

Tardy, *International Hallmarks on Silver Collected by Tardy*, Paris, 1981

Also useful, though not as easy to find or to use, unless you are familiar with German, is: M. Rosenberg, *Der Goldschmiede Merkzeichen*, Frankfurt, 1922–8.

It might be a good idea to have a quick glance at these volumes, before showing your work to an expert. Charles Truman recounts that while working at Christie's he was rung up by people who claimed with great excitement that their priceless piece of antique silver was signed with the initial of its maker: E.P.N.S., the acronym for Electro-Plated Nickel Silver. Half an hour in a library can help avoid such basic errors and save you any unnecessary embarrassment.

If you have managed to identify the mark, you will then be able to search for further details about the individual maker, and consult relevant publications for information about silver of the period and for illustrations of comparative pieces. Do not spend too much time on initial research, however. Better to go to an 'expert witness', who will be able to assess your work and point you in the right direction for further investigations.

Bibliography

Blair, Claude (ed). *The History of Silver*, London, Macdonald, 1987

Brett, Vanessa (ed). *The Sotheby's Directory of Silver, 1600–1940*, London, Sotheby's Publications, 1986

Clayton, Michael. *Christie's Pictorial History of English and American Silver*, London, Phaidon Christie's, 1985
   The Collector's Dictionary of the Silver and Gold of Great Britain and North America, Woodbridge, Antique Collectors' Club, 1985
Culme, John. *Nineteenth Century Silver*, London, Country Life Books, 1977

📖 **FURTHER ENQUIRIES AND SPECIALIST LIBRARIES**
If the 'Town' mark on your object is that of one of the four extant Assay Offices, then they might be able to help with advice. If it refers to one of the now defunct offices – for example, Chester or Exeter – contact the local museum to see if they have specialised in works by local silversmiths.

Assay Offices

The Assay Office
Goldsmiths' Hall
Gutter Lane
London EC2V 8AQ
Tel: 071 606 8971

The Assay Office
Newhall Street
Birmingham B3 1SB
Tel: 021 236 6951

The Assay Office
137 Portobello Street
Sheffield S1 4DR
Tel: 0742 755 111

The Assay Office
9 Granton Road
Edinburgh EH5 3QJ
Tel: 031 551 2189

The Assay Offices will be able to help you with the identification of British hallmarks generally and can supply information about the legal requirements governing precious metals.

Goldsmiths' Hall, above, also houses Goldsmiths' Library, a good place for works of reference and general enquiries.

Goldsmiths' Library
Goldsmiths' Hall
Foster Lane
London EC2V 6BN
Tel: 071 606 7010
Mon–Fri: 10–5, by appointment

The library houses a general collection of books and magazines related to silver, and also holds the records of the Goldsmiths' Company from the seventeenth century to the present day. It is particularly helpful for hallmarks and items relating to the Goldsmiths' Company and the London Assay Office.

If your object is connected with any particular body or corporation, or if it bears any specific symbols – for example, masonic – a relevant museum, society, or if still extant, the corporation itself, might be able to assist in your investigations (see also chapters 2 and 23). For identifying coats of arms and crests, refer to chapter 7. Should the work prove to have belonged to a person, house or institution of any importance, you might be able to trace an inventory or other papers connected with the piece (see chapter 3).

In certain circumstances, silver will be very well recorded. Charles Truman describes searching through Queen Anne's records for silver in the Lord Chamberlain's Accounts at the Public Record Office, where the last item he came across was the silver plate engraved for the Queen's coffin.

Should your piece be decorated with some form of narrative picture, you might be able to identify the scene and trace the original illustration from which it was taken. The Department of Prints and Drawings at the British Museum, and other museums mentioned in chapter 8 might be able to help you. A further possibly useful source of information could be the Department of Coins and Medals at museums such as the British Museum and the Ashmolean, where the curators might have come across a similar image in their own field.

✍ III. Expert Witnesses: Museums and Miscellaneous Sources

For specialist advice consult the museums and institutions listed below or go to an auction house or a good dealer. Do not be put off by the large uniformed doormen that you see in many silver shops: they are not there to keep you out, but to keep the silver in.

🏛 **MUSEUMS GENERAL**

Many museums and collections house important displays of silver. Those specifically recommended to me by expert witnesses in the field include:

The Victoria & Albert Museum, London

The Metalwork Department at the V&A is widely touted as perhaps the best place for enquiries about old silver. The department has a photographic archive open by appointment to serious researchers, and they can also supply helpful bibliographies. They hold an opinion service on Tuesday afternoons, 2.30–4.30. In addition to silver, silver plate, Sheffield plate, and so forth, the department also covers European and Islamic works of decorative art in metal from 500 AD to the present day, including: arms and armour, brass, candlesticks, candelabra, chandeliers and light fittings, chalices, church plate, crosses, clocks (in metal cases only), copper, cutlery, damascening, enamels, firebacks, ironwork, jewellery, keys, lead, ormolu, pewter, picqué, reliquaries in metal, snuff-boxes, steel and watches.

Other highly recommended collections of silver and possible sources of advice include: Manchester City Art Gallery; Temple Newsam House, Leeds; and the Ashmolean Museum, Oxford.

🏛 **MUSEUMS WITH IMPORTANT COLLECTIONS OF REGIONAL SILVER**

BIRMINGHAM SILVER AND SILVER GENERAL
Birmingham City Museum and Art Gallery

CHESTER–ASSAYED SILVER
Grosvenor Museum, Chester

EXETER SILVER
Royal Albert Memorial Museum, Exeter

NORWICH SILVER
Norwich Castle Museum

SHEFFIELD PLATE AND SILVER
Sheffield City Museum

The museum specialises in cutlery, silver and old Sheffield plate. The library is open by appointment and holds some archives, although the city's main collection of archives is in Sheffield's Libraries Department. Consultations are available by appointment and by post.

IRISH SILVER AND SILVER GENERAL
National Museum of Ireland, Dublin

Ulster Museum, Belfast

SCOTTISH SILVER AND SILVER GENERAL
Glasgow Art Gallery and Museum

Royal Museum of Scotland, Edinburgh

14
Clocks, Watches and Scientific Instruments

Clocks and Watches

✍ I. EXAMINE THE EVIDENCE

Measure and photograph the object and assemble any provenance information (see Part One). Examine the work closely and try to compile a basic description of the material, design and decoration. Look at the overall shape, and individual parts such as the face and hands.

One of the advantages of investigating clocks and watches is that they are frequently signed – a blessed relief to the art detective. Look for the signature on the dial or the movement. This will tell you the name of the maker, the manufacturer or the retailer, which you can then look up in the horological bibles listed below.

Transcribe any written information or marks that you find. Hallmarked watch cases can provide a useful means of identification (see chapter 13); but just as you cannot judge a book by its cover, so you should not assess a watch by its case. Two gold watches could appear almost identical from the outside, but one might be worth £2,000 and the other £20,000, because of what it contains – the movement can easily be the more important element.

A clock case, while it can help you to date a piece stylistically, is unlikely to be signed or marked. Though a knowledge of furniture history will give you some idea of its period, it is important to remember that an old case is no guarantee of an old movement.

According to Tina Miller, director of the Clocks and Watches Department at Sotheby's, some of the most common problems found on items brought for assessment include movements that have been changed, hands that are of a later date than the clock itself, replaced dials on pocket watches and, generally, 'bits missing'. The name of a well-known maker could have been inscribed on a period clock to make it more collectable. The art detective should beware of marriages of different movements and cases, and of nineteenth-century copies of sixteenth- and seventeenth-century pocket watches. Such horological skulduggery was not restricted to the Victorian era. Jeremy Evans, clock expert at the British Museum, notes that even in the seventeenth-century fakes were a problem, with members of the Clockmakers Company complaining bitterly about the importation of watches falsely bearing the names of London makers.

Without some form of experience in the field, it is impossible to assess the mechanism and inner workings of your clock or watch. Beyond opening it up to look for a name, leave any further speculation to the experts. Obviously, a beginner cannot be expected to spot criminal refinements, but there are plenty of experienced detectives who can (see below). If you suspect something is wrong with your piece, do not try to put it right yourself. Also, do not give it a particularly enthusiastic clean just because you are about to show it off. Academics and dealers alike would prefer to see dirty rather than damaged goods, and modern restorations only make the article more complicated to read.

✍ II. The Investigation

📖 **LIBRARY RESEARCH AND BASIC REFERENCE BOOKS**
For looking up the name of your maker, the following books
are recommended:

ENGLISH AND INTERNATIONAL
Britten, F. J. *Old Clocks and Watches and their Makers*, 9th ed,
    London, Methuen & Co, 1982
Loomes, Brian. *Watchmakers and Clockmakers of the World*, vol
    2, 2nd ed, Ipswich, N.A.G. Press, 1978

FRENCH
Tardy, H. L. *Dictionnaire des Horlogers Français*, 2 vols, Paris,
    1972

GERMAN
Abeler, Jurgen. *Meister der Uhrmacherkunst*, 1977

Check through the library's catalogue for any other books
that might be useful. If you are investigating a particular type
of clock or watch, look for a relevant specialist publication.
The Antique Collectors' Club has produced a number of
excellent horological monographs on the subject in general
and on specific areas, including lantern clocks, longcase clocks,
and carriage clocks. Many books have also been written
about clockmakers of a specific town or country. For checking
hallmarks, see the silver bibliography in chapter 13, and for
assessing your clock case, refer to chapter 10 on furniture.

✍ III. Expert Witnesses: Museums and Miscellaneous Sources

Perhaps the best place in Britain for identifications, specialist
advice and generally embarking upon your investigations is
the Horological Students' Room, at the British Museum.

Horological Students' Room
British Museum, London
Tel: 071 636 1555 ext 8395
Mon–Fri: 10.30–4.45 (telephone for an appointment)

The Students' Room epitomises the superb behind-the-scenes services provided by our national museums, which, sadly, are being increasingly threatened by cutbacks. It houses a magnificent study collection of pocket-watches, from the late sixteenth-century timepiece to the digital watch, and a fine display of clocks. At the time of writing, there is a staff of four experts who can help you with enquiries about specific items and point you in the right direction for your studies. For the clock detective at whatever level, the British Museum provides an invaluable centre of reference and a unique opportunity to talk to experts.

🏛 **MUSEUMS GENERAL**

A short selection of museums and institutions holding material relating to clocks and watches is listed below; also refer to the museums in the scientific instruments section. For information concerning provincial clockmakers, try contacting the relevant regional museum or record office.

London

CLOCKS GENERAL
The Victoria & Albert Museum

FRENCH CLOCKS
The Wallace Collection

LONDON CLOCKMAKERS
Library & Collection of the Worshipful Company of
    Clockmakers
The Clock Room
Guildhall Library

London was a major clockmaking centre. There is an important collection of clocks at the Guildhall, and the library holds the records of the Clockmakers' Company, established in London in 1631. While some of these archives have been published (The Company of Clockmakers. *Register of Apprentices 1631–1931*, London, 1931), much information may still be gleaned by the serious student who is prepared to return to the source and decipher period handwriting.

Regional

CLOCKS GENERAL

Herbert Art Gallery and Museum, Coventry

The museum's collection includes watches and clocks, as well as books, pamphlets and archive material on the ribbon and watch trades.

Usher Gallery, Lincoln

The gallery holds an important horological collection, particularly strong in watches. Consultations are available on Tuesday afternoons and Friday mornings.

CLOCKS GENERAL AND SUFFOLK CLOCKMAKERS

The Clock Museum, Bury St Edmunds

The museum specialises in German and English clocks, American horology, turret clocks and European watches from the seventeenth to the twentieth centuries. The library is open by appointment, and the archives include material on Suffolk clocks and clockmakers. Objects can be brought in for examination on Wednesday afternoons.

LANCASHIRE WATCH TRADES

Prescot Museum of Clock and Watchmaking

The history of horology, particularly the Lancashire watch trades and the Lancashire Watch Company, is the focus of the Prescot Museum's collection. The museum library holds archives for both the craftsmen and the factories represented in the collection, and is open to the public by appointment. Consultations are also available by appointment and by post, and material can be left for assessment at the museum.

LEICESTERSHIRE CLOCKMAKERS

Newarke Houses Museum, Leicester

The museum, a sixteenth-century chantry house and a seventeenth-century dwelling house, specialises in Leicestershire history, including works by local clockmakers. Its archives include material concerning the Deacon family of clockmakers. The library is open by appointment, and an identification service is provided on request.

✉ USEFUL ADDRESSES AND SPECIALIST SOCIETIES

The British Horological Institute
Upton Hall
Upton
Newark
Notts NT23 5TE
Tel: 0636 813 795

Along with many other services, the institute houses a museum open to the public on certain days and one of the best horological libraries in the world. Phone for details.

The Antiquarian Horological Society
Newhouse
High Street
Ticehurst
Wadhurst
Sussex TN5 7AL
Tel: 0580 200155

✉ EXISTING COMPANIES

If the firm that made your watch or timepiece is still in existence, it might be worthwhile writing to the company to see if they hold any archives or information. As a general rule, the posher the label, the better your chances.

For Audemars Piguet contact: Audemars Piguet, Manufacture d'Horlogerie, CH 1348, Le Brassus, Switzerland. For information on the Breguet archives write to: Breguet, 25 Chemin Creux de Corsay, 1093 La Conversion, Lausanne, Switzerland.

Cartier keep archives in London, Paris and New York, dating from the foundation of the company to the present day. For further information contact the Cartier Archives Department, Cartier Ltd, 175 New Bond Street, London W1Y 0QA, Tel: 071 493 6962. For information on works by Chaumet, contact the Chaumet Museum, 12 Place Vendome, 75001 Paris.

The Swiss watchmakers Patek have preserved their records, and if you want to find out the original details of your piece, their UK distributors, Rhone Products, will contact the Patek archives in Switzerland on your behalf. Write to: Rhone Products UK, PO Box 368, Harrow HA1 3LQ, Tel: 081 864 7620.

Scientific Instruments

✍ I. EXAMINE THE EVIDENCE

Submit your piece to the usual examination, note down any marks or signatures, take photographs and record the provenance. The first thing to establish is what the instrument is – not always the easiest question in this strange and varied field. If you do not know yourself, you will have to turn to a book or an expert witness, such as a museum, reputable dealer or auction house (see Part One).

✍ II. THE INVESTIGATION

📖 LIBRARY RESEARCH AND BASIC REFERENCE BOOKS

A good beginner's introduction to the field of scientific instruments is: Harriet Wynter and Anthony John Turner, *Scientific Instruments* (London, Studio Vista Publishers, 1975).

Other useful general works containing information about instruments and their makers include:

Brevington, M. V. *The Peabody Museum of Collecting of Scientific Instruments*, Salem, Massachusetts, 1963

Daumas, Maurice. *Scientific Instruments of the 17th and 18th Century and their Makers*, London, B. T. Batsford, 1972

National Maritime Museum. *An Inventory of the Navigation and Astronomy Collections in the National Maritime Museum*, Greenwich, National Maritime Museum, 1970

Taylor, Eva Germaine R. *The Mathematical Practitioners of Tudor and Stuart England*, Cambridge, Cambridge University Press, 1954

Mathematical Practitioners of Hanoverian England 1714–1840, Cambridge, Cambridge University Press, 1966

Tooley, Ronald Vere (ed). *Tooley's Dictionary of Map Makers*, Tring, 1979 (supplement 1985)

Turner, Gerard L'Estrange. *Antique Scientific Instruments*, London, Blandford Press, 1980
Nineteenth Century Scientific Instruments, London, Sotheby Publications, 1983

Specialist Bibliography

BAROMETERS

Banfield, Edwin. *Barometers*, 3 vols, Trowbridge, Baros Books, 1985

Goodison, Nicholas. *English Barometers 1680–1860*, London, Cassell & Co, 1969

GLOBES

Der Globusfreund (journal)

Stevenson, E. L. *Terrestrial and Celestial Globes*, New York, Hispanic Society of America, 1921

van der Krogt, P. *Old Globes in the Netherlands*, Utrecht, 1984

MICROSCOPES

Turner, Gerard L'Estrange. *Collecting Microscopes*, London, Studio Vista Publications, 1981
The Great Age of the Microscope: The Collection of the Royal Microscopical Society, 150 Years, Bristol, Hilger, 1989

SEXTANTS

Cotter, C. H. *The Divided Circle: A History of the Navigator's Sextant*, Glasgow, Brown, Son & Ferguson, 1985

📖 **FURTHER ENQUIRIES AND SPECIALIST LIBRARIES**

For more in-depth investigations you will have to look for contemporaneous material, such as commercial and exhibition catalogues. Period trade cards can be a helpful source of research and often bear fine illustrations of instruments produced by the maker. The Science Museum in London has a major collection of historical trade cards (see Calvert, H. R.

Scientific Trade Cards in the Science Museum Collection, London, HMSO, 1971).

If you are working on a particular maker or manufacturer, it is always worth checking to see if the individual or firm has ever published anything, such as a description of their works or a learned paper on some related topic. While these might or might not provide you with precise details on your particular object, they can certainly yield fascinating background information.

I once had to research a pair of handsome library globes by the celebrated eighteenth-century globemaker John Senex. In 1718 Senex published a treatise on the use of globes in which, along with a contemporary pricelist, he included his own socio-geographical survey of the world. While Britain and Ireland were ranked in first place, 'for that either in Salubrity of Air, Plenty of all Things necessary to Humane Life, or other Advantages, they need not give place to any Country in the Universe', other races and countries fared less well. The Italians 'though kind to strangers are yet inclined to Jealousies, Wantonness and Sharp Revenge'; German women are written off as being 'somewhat Corpulent' and of 'Indifferent Complexion'; in France 'the people are generally Complemental, Inconstant and Rash – They feed most on boil'd or liquid meats and are very curious in Sauces'.

Although this distinctly biased account told me nothing about the globes themselves, it nevertheless offered an insight into Senex and his period, bringing the man to life and providing an amusing picture of the attitudes of a successful cartographer and globemaker in Hanoverian Britain.

To continue with globes: globe-stands, the legs or supports upon which the library globe rests, are often wonderful examples of period craftsmanship and fall into the province of the furniture detective rather than the scientist. A comprehensive introduction to the subject is provided in *The Dictionary of English Furniture* (Woodbridge, Antique Collectors' Club, 1983) and advice should be sought from the furniture specialist.

Generally speaking, when you are investigating scientific instruments, you will require the facilities of a major national library, or a good scientific library. The latter is probably the better choice, since staff will be able to offer you specialist advice and the collections are more likely to include archival material that could be relevant to your enquiries.

All the museums listed below have libraries, and other useful institutions include:

The British Library
Science Reference and Information Service
25 Southampton Buildings
London WC2A 1AW
Tel: 071 323 7494 (general enquiries)
Mon–Fri: 9.30–9; Sat: 10–1

SRIS covers a broad range of subjects relating to science, technology and business, and has reading rooms at three different sites. Phone General Enquiries to establish which section you will need.

The Royal Society
6 Carlton House Terrace
London SW1Y 5AG
Tel: 071 839 5561
Library, Mon–Fri: 10–7

Founded in 1660, the Royal Society is an independent learned society for the promotion of natural sciences, including mathematics and all applied aspects such as engineering and medicine. The library and archives form an important resource for research into the history and development of science since 1660 and for current publications. Data on Fellows and books by Fellows and foreign members are collected, as are journals of science academies worldwide. There is a large collection of photographic and illustrated material. While the library is mainly for the use of society members, other readers are welcomed.

🐾 III. EXPERT WITNESSES: MUSEUMS AND MISCELLANEOUS SOURCES

🏛 MUSEUMS FOR SCIENTIFIC INSTRUMENTS, CLOCKS AND WATCHES

London

National Maritime Museum, Greenwich

The National Maritime Museum houses the finest collection of navigational instruments in the world, as well as instruments and material connected with the history of astronomy, time determination, measurement, hydrography, etc. Comprehensive printed and archival material is available in the library.

National Museum of Science and Industry

Britain's Science Museum houses a collection of over 200,000 objects covering the fields of science, technology and industry. The building is also home to the Wellcome Museum of the History of Medicine. Consultations are available by appointment. The museum's library (Tel: 071 938 8284) is a national scientific and technical library, and its vast collection of books and periodicals includes most of the important works published in the field since the fifteenth century. General reference material includes full sets of British patents, London directories, international exhibition catalogues, and a substantial holding of trade literature. There is an important pictorial and archive collection. The library is open to the public, but a reader's ticket must be obtained to consult special material and old and rare books.

Regional

Museum of the History of Science, Oxford

The museum has an unrivalled collection of early astronomical, surveying and mathematical instruments, and the largest collection of astrolabes in the world. There is a fine display of clocks and watches, and optical collections include early telescopes, microscopes and photographic apparatus. Consultations are available by appointment. The library is open to readers by arrangement with the librarian. The extensive manuscript collection includes the H. E. Stapleton Archive relating to Islamic alchemy and there is an important collection of printed material and related ephemera: prints and photographs of scientists, scientific instrument makers and apparatus; drawings, paintings, handbills, etc.

Whipple Museum of the History of Science, Cambridge

The collection includes scientific instruments from the Renaissance to the present day, and is particularly strong in traditional mathematical instruments, including sundials, quadrants and astrolabes, surveying instruments and microscopes. Consultations are available by appointment, and the library is open by prior application.

15

Costume, Textiles, Oriental Rugs and Carpets

Perhaps the first thing to say about investigating old textiles is that the material evidence should be handled with extreme care. Beware of rings and bracelets that could catch a thread and cause damage, and remember that strong light is harmful. The Costume Museum at Bath recommends that when lifting a textile or costume, both hands should be used to ensure adequate support. Never pick up a piece by a single corner, since this can cause undue strain on seams and fibres. If you want to preserve the quality of an antique item of dress, do not – however tempting it may be – try it on.

Do not try to clean fabrics without professional advice and the same goes for repairs. 'You wouldn't believe the number of tapestries that I've seen darned like a pair of socks,' one leading textile dealer told me indignantly. 'Some people even stick backings on with glue, which damages the piece and destroys its value. Criminal behaviour!'

For storing or wrapping up your item use either acid-free tissue paper (available from most good stationers), or a clean white cotton sheet. Roll tapestries and carpets rather than fold them.

The field of textiles is as wide as it is specialised, encompassing everything from a pair of Victorian knickers to a priceless medieval tapestry. Since this chapter rashly attempts to deal with the subject as a whole, I shall concentrate predominantly on recommending certain useful books and centres of expertise. From these sources you will be able to gather the technical information needed to assess your object and to track down its history. Refer to Part One for more general information about conducting your investigation.

Costume, Textiles and Carpets

✍ I. EXAMINE THE EVIDENCE

Whatever your object, be it costume, textile or carpet, examine it closely and measure it if it seems relevant (i.e. do not measure a glove but do measure a carpet or tapestry). Collect any known provenance information and if the object is not easily portable, take photographs.

Try to answer the following questions:

What is it?
Does it appear hand– or machine-made and how has it been put together?
What material is it made from?
Can you make a rough guess, or do you have any information as to where it comes from? Is it Eastern or Western?
How is it decorated and/or worked?
Is there a mark, label or signature?
Are there any additional details or miscellaneous elements that you should note?

Compile as full a description as you can for your object, so that you can begin to understand it, and thus identify the right books to use and the best specialists to consult.

✍ II. The Investigation

📖 LIBRARY RESEARCH AND BASIC REFERENCE BOOKS

You will need to go to a good art history library for investigations in this field. Many books will simply not be available elsewhere and, without some form of advice, it is not always easy for the amateur detective to distinguish serious works of reference from the disposable, coffee table antiques books that are published in the thousands. When researching a newspaper article on Oriental carpets, I found three books on the subject in my local library. When I showed them to a carpet specialist, his response was unequivocal: 'You can't use those, they are complete crap and full of factual errors.'

A good art library will offer you a wide choice of material, and you will be able to ask the librarian for assistance. Consult the catalogue for works on your subject, and remember to be both general and specific in your enquiries: for example, if you are researching underwear, look up the subject in general books on costume history, not just in specific monographs on underclothes. Similarly, information on furnishing textiles is often to be found in books on furniture, furnishings and the decorative arts as a whole.

A number of the museums listed below will have libraries, and some, such as the Department of Textile Furnishings and Dress at the V&A, will supply bibliographies, free of charge, on a wide range of costume and textile subjects. As a starting-off point, however, the works listed below have all been recommended to me as either good beginner's books or standard bibles.

CARPETS GENERAL

Bennett, Ian (ed). *The Book of Rugs and Carpets of the World*, London, Country Life Books, 1978

Black, David. *World Rugs and Carpets*, London, Newnes Books, 1985

Faraday, Cornelia Bateman. *European and American Carpets and Rugs*, Woodbridge, Antique Collectors' Club, 1990

See also Oriental Rugs and Carpets, page 160.

COSTUME AND DRESS

For investigating costume, there are two extremely useful guides: Janet Arnold's *Handbook of Costume* (London, Macmillan, 1973) and Valerie Cumming's *Exploring Costume History 1500–1900* (London, Batsford Educational, 1981). Both authors offer comprehensive advice on how to conduct historical research and how to use the museums, libraries and record offices available. Janet Arnold is particularly and practically informative on all the different sources available to the costume detective, covering everything from paintings, to dolls, to construction techniques; she also provides a good bibliography and a comprehensive guide to costume collections in the British Isles.

A short bibliography of helpful general works on costume includes:

D'Allemagne, H. R. *Les Accessoires du Costume et du Mobilier depuis le treizième jusqu'au milieu du dix-neuvième siècle*, Paris, Schemit, 1928 (a good book on costume accessories)

Anthony, P. and Arnold, Janet (eds). *Costume: A General Bibliography*, London, Costume Society Publications Department, 1974

von Boehn, M. *Modes and Manners* (a series of books published by Harrap between 1927 and 1935, and covering fashion 'From the Decline of the ancient world . . .' to the nineteenth century)

Boucher, François. *A History of Costume in the West*, London, Thames & Hudson, 1983 (according to the Fashion Research Centre at Bath, this is the most used of all their general encyclopaedias)

Davenport, M. *The Book of Costume*, New York, 1948

Kelly, F. M. and Schwabe, R. *Historic Costume: A Chronicle of Fashion in Western Europe 1490–1790*, London, 1925

EMBROIDERY AND NEEDLEWORK

Schuette, M. and Muller-Christensen, S. *The Art of Embroidery*, London, Thames & Hudson, 1964

Sebba, Anne. *Samplers: Five Centuries of a Gentle Craft*, London, Weidenfeld & Nicolson, 1979

Staniland, K. *Medieval Craftsmen–Embroiderers*, London, British Museum Publications, 1991

Synge, Lanto. *Antique Needlework*, London, Blandford Press, 1989

Synge, Lanto (ed). *The Royal School of Needlework Book of Needlework and Embroidery*, London, Collins, 1986

LACE

Kraatz, Anne. *Lace: History and Fashion*, London, Thames & Hudson, 1989

Levey, Santina. *Lace: A History*, London, Victoria & Albert Museum, 1983

TAPESTRIES

Examine the main picture of the tapestry, since its style will help you to determine the date. Note down the subject matter, which could be anything from a classical drama to a peasant festival to an entirely formal design. If the subject portrayed is figurative, you might possibly be able to track down the original work from which it was taken (see chapter 8). Take note of the borders, since their design can be very important in determining questions of date and workshop; sometimes they will contain the mark of the factory or the weaver.

Recommended works on tapestries include:

Digby, G. Wingfield. *V&A Museum, The Tapestry Collection – Medieval and Renaissance*, London, HMSO, 1980

Goebel, H. *Wandteppiche*, 6 vols, Leipzig, Verlag von Klinkhardt & Biermann, 1923–34 (the tapestry bible)

Heinz, Dora. *Tapestries of Europe and of Colonial Peru in the Museum of Fine Arts, Boston*, 2 vols, Boston, 1967

Marillier, H. C. *English Tapestries of the 18th Century*, London, 1930

✍ III. Expert Witnesses: Museums and Miscellaneous Sources

Many museums have collections devoted to costume and textiles, so it might be worth enquiring at your local museum before approaching one of the major institutions. Whether you wish to use a museum for an identification service or to study primary source material from their collections, always make an appointment. For a more comprehensive guide to costume collections in Britain, consult Janet Arnold, see page 151. Museums with collections of ethnographic textiles are listed in chapter 19. For general purposes, the Victoria & Albert Museum is a good place to begin your investigations, while Bath holds the most important costume collection in Britain and is perhaps the main centre for fashion research.

🏛 MUSEUMS

London

ARTS AND CRAFTS TEXTILES
William Morris Gallery

COSTUMES, CARPETS AND TEXTILES GENERAL
The Victoria & Albert Museum
Department of Textile Furnishings and Dress

The V&A is one of the best jumping-off points for all kinds of textile-related investigation. There are fine collections of carpets and costume, and a wonderful textile study collection on open display. The department holds an opinion service on Tuesday afternoons, 2.30–4.30.

FANS
The Fan Museum

This is the only museum in the world devoted exclusively to fan-making. The collection is particularly strong in European fans from the eighteenth and nineteenth centuries, and covers its subject from early examples through to the present day. Consultations are available by appointment.

SILVER STUDIO TEXTILES AND WALLPAPERS
Silver Studio Collection

Founded by Arthur Silver in 1880, the Silver Studio became Britain's largest commercial design studio, remaining active until 1963. Its complete contents are preserved by the museum; the collection of late nineteenth- and early twentieth-century textiles and wallpapers is one of the most important in Europe. The library is open to the public by appointment. As well as journals and trade catalogues, the museum preserves the archives of Arthur Silver, Charles Hasler and George Jack.

Regional

AMERICAN TEXTILES, QUILTS
The American Museum in Britain, Bath

CARPETS
Kidderminster Museum and Art Gallery

The museum specialises in carpets of the nineteenth and twentieth centuries, with related objects and documentation. At the time of writing, the museum is closed to the public pending the purchase of new premises, but postal enquiries are still answered and the collection can be opened for serious researchers. Telephone 0562 66610 for details.

COSTUME AND DRESS
Devonshire Collection of Period Costume, Totnes

This private collection staffed by volunteers specialises in costume from the eighteenth to the twentieth centuries. There is a reference library open by request; identifications are available by appointment and by post.

Museum of Costume, Bath

The museum holds one of the largest and most comprehensive collections of costume in Britain, covering fashionable dress for men, women and children from the late sixteenth century to the present day. Consultations are on Thursday and Friday afternoons by appointment, and enquiries can be made by post. The museum includes a reserve collection for research, but its library, archives and main study collection are to be found at the:

Fashion Research Centre, Bath

The library holds books, patterns, illustrations, periodicals and photographs. There is much primary source material from the nineteenth and twentieth centuries; the archives include the records of Worth and Paquin and other fashion houses, as well as the *Sunday Times* Fashion Archive 1957–72. The study collection of costume accessories, textiles and needlework extends from the eighteenth to the twentieth centuries. The centre offers a consultation service on Thursdays and Fridays between 2.15 and 3.15. Identifications are given, as well as advice on the care and conservation of textiles. Appointments must be made in writing.

St John's House, Warwick

The museum specialises in costume, dolls and toys. There is a costume study room open by special request (Tel: 0926 412021), which includes catalogues, drawings and patterns. Identifications can be made by appointment and by letter, but always telephone before visiting.

COSTUME AND LACE
Rougemont House Museum of Costume and Lace, Exeter

The museum specialises in costume from 1750 to the present day, and includes a collection of Continental and English lace that concentrates particularly on East Devon Honiton lace. There is a related library which holds some lace sample books. Consultations are available on Thursdays, 2–5, but phone for an appointment before visiting.

COSTUME AND TEXTILES GENERAL
The Bowes Museum, Barnard Castle

The museum is strong in both textiles and costume. The textile collection includes an important tapestry display, needlework, embroideries, carpets, quilts, and a good selection of French upholstery textiles of the seventeenth and eighteenth centuries. Consultations are available by appointment. The museum's library is open to the public on Thursday, 2–5, and Saturday, 10–12.

The Gallery of English Costume, Manchester

One of the largest costume museums in the country, the museum specialises in British and European clothes from the seventeenth century to the present day, and dress accessories and 'everything to do with the care and adornment of the person'. It also houses collections of textiles and embroideries from the Western world and the East. The museum offers fine research facilities. Its library, open to researchers by appointment, contains some 180,000 items, including nineteenth- and twentieth-century fashion magazines, as well as trade and shop catalogues. Identifications can be made by appointment.

Stoke-on-Trent City Museum and Art Gallery

The gallery's collections of decorative art include a fine display of costume from the eighteenth to the twentieth centuries. The archives include documentary photographs of dress from the 1880s onwards, and a collection of pattern books. Consultations are available by appointment and by post.

COSTUME, TEXTILES AND LACE
Museum of Costume and Textiles, Nottingham

The museum specialises in costume and textiles, but its primary focus is on lace and the Nottingham lace trade (machine-made lace). The collection's reference library can be viewed by appointment. The museum holds archive material and sample books relating to local firms, lace and embroidery companies. Consultations are available by appointment and by post, but include a self-addressed stamped envelope with your letter.

LACE
Allhallows Museum, Honiton

The town museum holds Britain's most important collection of Honiton lace. Consultations about lace are available by appointment or by post.

LEATHER
Northampton Museum of Leathercraft

The museum specialises in the history of leathercraft and its library is open to the public by appointment.

RIBBONS AND COSTUME
Herbert Art Gallery and Museum, Coventry

The museum houses a costume section and a national collection of silk ribbons. Archives include material on the ribbon and watch trades, and the library is open by appointment. Objects may be left for identification; consultations are available by appointment and by post.

SHOES
The Shoe Museum, Somerset

The museum is devoted to the history of shoe manufacture. There is a small library, and enquiries can be made by appointment.

Northampton Central Museum and Art Gallery

The museum houses a boot and shoe collection of national importance, and a fine display of leathercraft. A reference library concerning both of these subjects can be consulted by special request. Enquiries can be made by appointment and by post.

TEXTILES GENERAL, COPTIC TEXTILES, WALLPAPERS
Whitworth Art Gallery, Manchester

The gallery houses an extensive collection of textiles from the Egyptian period to the present day. It is international in scope and includes a remarkable group of Coptic textiles. Another strength is its collection of wallpapers from the seventeenth century to the present day. The library is open to the public by prior arrangement, and the archive collection on wallpaper is particularly good. Consultations are available by appointment on the last Thursday of every month.

TEXTILES
Fitzwilliam Museum, Cambridge

Northern Ireland

IRISH LACE AND COSTUME GENERAL
Ulster Museum, Belfast

Republic of Ireland
IRISH LACE AND COSTUME GENERAL
National Museum of Ireland, Dublin

Scotland

TARTANS AND HIGHLAND DRESS
Scottish Tartans Society and Museum, Comrie
The society holds the register of all publicly known tartans and is the centre of expertise on Highland dress. There is an extensive archive and a research department, which, for a fee, provides identifications of tartans and advice on all matters concerning Scottish costume and clan history as related to tartans.

The West Highland Museum, Fort William
The museum houses a general local collection and specialises in Jacobite and tartan material. The library can be consulted by special request; enquiries are accepted by appointment and by post.

TEXTILES AND COSTUME
Royal Museum of Scotland, Edinburgh
The museum houses an important collection of costume and textiles, both Scottish and international, and is responsible for Shambellie House Museum of Costume which specialises in European costume from the eighteenth to the twentieth centuries.

TEXTILES, TAPESTRIES AND CARPETS
Burrell Collection, Glasgow
The collection includes textiles, tapestries, and one of the most important collections of Eastern carpets in the British Isles.

✉ **USEFUL ADDRESSES**

Needlework, Embroidery and Textiles

Embroiderers' Guild
Apartment 41
Hampton Court Palace
East Molesey
Surrey KT8 9AU
Tel: 081 943 1229

The Embroiderers' Guild is a charitable trust founded in 1906 to promote the craft of embroidery through workshops, lectures and a whole range of activities. The guild owns a major collection of historic and modern embroideries, and houses an important library. Telephone for details about membership and using the facilities.

Royal School of Needlework
Apartment 12A
Hampton Court Palace
Tel: 081 943 1432

A centre of expertise on needlework, both antique and modern, the work of the school includes both the care and preservation of antique textiles and the creation of new works of art.

Textile Conservation Centre
Apartment 22
Base Court
Hampton Court Palace
Tel: 081 977 4943

The Textile Conservation Centre concentrates on the conservation of all kinds of historic textiles and the training of conservators.

Oriental Carpets and Rugs

It takes years of study and experience to unravel the mysteries of Oriental carpets and rugs, nevertheless there are a few clues that the amateur detective can follow (also see Part One).

✍ I. EXAMINE THE EVIDENCE

Look at your rug, measure it, and compile all the basic provenance details. The first thing you will need to establish is whether or not your rug is hand-made (i.e. hand-knotted). Turn it over: if the reverse shows a clearly defined pattern and strong colours, it is likely to be hand-made. Examine the front of the rug for slight irregularities: machine-made rugs often look mechanical.

For a rug to be collectable, it is also important that it should be dyed with a vegetable as opposed to chemical dyes. Here again, only experience or an expert can enable you to reach any certain conclusions, but the specialists I consulted came up with a few pointers. Look for variations in tone within a single colour, which might have emerged as the weaver gradually worked through the carpet. Known in the trade as 'abrash', these colour changes occur particularly with natural dyes and in rural rugs. For the enthusiast, these are not imperfections but part of the unique personality of a rug. 'You can get the most wonderful movement of colours,' explains dealer Clive Loveless, 'they really bring a rug to life. Uniform tones appear flat and dead by comparison.'

Contrary to what one might expect, faded colours do not necessarily mean an old carpet, but tend to suggest that it has been chemically dyed. Chemical dyes are more fugitive and often prone to bleeding, particularly certain red and orange tones. 'Look for ivory areas of a carpet, and see if the colours have run into it,' advises Loveless. Another test, although by no means infallible, is to spit on a handkerchief and rub hard on the possibly offending colours. If the handkerchief stains, the dyes are likely to be chemical; some natural dyes will also run but only slightly in comparison.

Look at the material, the weave and the design. Much has been written about the meanings of patterns in carpets, and many books produce a comprehensive interpretation of symbols. However, it is an area that the amateur detective should approach with caution, since ultimately there are as many possible interpretations as there are people to make them.

Though most rugs are anonymous, some examples will be signed and/or dated in Arabic numerals and according to the Moslem calendar. Dates are not necessarily foolproof, because they could have been faked or simply copied by a weaver from another rug as part and parcel of the general design, so be cautious.

II. THE INVESTIGATION

LIBRARY RESEARCH AND BASIC REFERENCE BOOKS

Many books and guides of extremely varying quality have been written about rugs and carpets. Clive Loveless offers the following advice: 'Before getting your knickers in a twist about details and reference books, look at and live with your rug, get some sort of feeling for its quality and colour – a good old rug has a life of its own.'

Alan Marcuson, editor of *Hali* magazine (see below) agrees: 'There's an old dealer's saying: "you buy carpets with your eyes and not with your ears". The same is true for learning about carpets and reading books about them: in many instances you would do better ignoring the text and concentrating on the photographs.'

Nevertheless, the one book that everyone recommends as a good introduction to Oriental carpets is: Jon Thompson *Carpets from the Tents, Cottages and Workshops of Asia: An Introduction* (London, Barrie & Jenkins, 1988). Thompson provides a clear and beautifully illustrated guide to understanding your object. Rather than categorising carpets by the country of origin – which can be extremely confusing as any individual country can produce many different styles – Thompson divides carpets and rugs into four basic categories: tribal weavings, cottage or village productions, town or city carpets, and court carpets. The system is both enlightening and easy to follow. The book includes substantial and readable information on all aspects of carpet lore: technical, historical, social, buying and selling ... It also contains a very good bibliography, and is an absolute must for the carpet detective.

Recommended books on Kilims:

Black, D. and Loveless, C. (eds). *The Undiscovered Kilim*, London, David Black Oriental Carpets, 1977
Cootner, Kathryn and Muse, Garry. *Anatolian Kilims*, London, Philip Wilson Publishers, 1989

For the latest research, news and information in the field of antique carpets and textiles, particularly Oriental carpets, a very useful and beautiful publication is *Hali – The International Magazine of Fine Carpets and Textiles* (Hali Publications, Kingsgate House, Kingsgate Place, London NW6 4TA, Tel: 071 328 9341). The annual subscription fee is £52.

✍ III. Expert Witnesses: Museums and Miscellaneous Sources

For advice on rugs, your best bet is to chat to a reputable dealer (consult BADA). Museums with good collections of rugs in Britain include: the V&A, London; the Ashmolean, Oxford; the Fitzwilliam, Cambridge; and the Burrell in Glasgow.

16
Toys and Dolls

According to the Collectables Department at Sotheby's, the most common mistake people make about toys is thinking that they are valuable. Not every ancient teddy bear, however much loved, is worth £50,000. Whatever your toy, its value is hugely affected by such factors as condition, accessories, and whether or not the original box has been preserved. If you were one of those children who never chipped toy soldiers, lost dolly's original clothes, and always put everything carefully back in its proper packaging, you could reap the benefits as an adult. More important than anything, however, is the innate rarity of the object itself.

To avoid disappointment, do not assume that the contents of your toybox are worth a fortune, but nevertheless treat them with respect. Consider what the object is made of and handle it accordingly: be gentle with fabrics, do not leave wax dolls in direct light, keep all accessories together, and put everything out of the way of the children.

If your toy or doll is in any way damaged, do not attempt to repair it yourself. An expert always prefers to see the object in its original state, and serious collectors would much rather carry out their own restoration. One museum curator told me with horror how he had seen a lovely Victorian doll's house, completely revamped in 1960s style with open plan living room, radiators instead of a fireplace, and all the doors made flush. Although fascinating as a reflection of modern domestic mores, it was disastrous for the antique collector. So leave everything in its natural state.

✍ I. EXAMINE THE EVIDENCE

As with all other antiques, begin your researches by examining the object (see Part One). Ask yourself the usual leading questions: what is it and what is it made of? Is there a stamp, mark or label, and does this suggest a nationality?

Measure the item, examine its composition, features and surface decoration, and write down any related family history: i.e. that it was given to Aunty Flo for her fifth birthday in 1905. If there is a box, record its information and be sure to keep any additional leaflets and accessories. Boxes are very important and can triple the value of a toy. In the field of model cars, for example, an original box on its own can command a certain price. The development of laser printing has led to fake packaging: even in such an apparently innocent field as toys, the art detective should still be on his or her guard against the art criminal.

As most toys were originally designed for little fingers, they are small enough to be portable, and you can take the object with you when you go in search of specialist advice. However, ensure that it is carefully packed. If there is any risk of damage or loss of individual parts, or if it is simply too big, take photographs instead.

✍ II. THE INVESTIGATION

📖 LIBRARY RESEARCH AND BASIC REFERENCE BOOKS

Collecting toys, games and dolls has become an increasingly popular activity for grown-ups. New books and monographs are continually being published, along with reprints of original catalogues, both from toy manufacturers and department stores such as Gamages, which can help with identifying and dating your toy. The best course is to consult your local art reference library, or a major national library.

Look up both the general subject and, where relevant, the make (e.g. Matchbox) to see if a book has been published on the firm that produced your piece. In a field this diverse and specialised, I can only offer a few elementary clues from specialists about what to look for in the object and a limited bibliography of useful publications. You will need to spend some time looking through the subject index in the library to find more detailed information about books and documents relating to your particular area. Don't forget that you can always go to the experts for suggestions and advice.

Dolls

With dolls, first try to establish what material your example is made of: bisque (ceramic), wax, wood, cloth, plastic. Take note of the features and the composition of the body. 'A closed mouth can suggest an early doll as can a fixed, as opposed to a swivel, wrist,' advises doll dealer Rachel Leigh.

Look for a mark: the most common place tends to be the back of the head or shoulders, although it can also be found on other parts of the body, such as the soles of the feet. Marks can be placed directly on the doll, or written, printed or embroidered in the form of labels. A name, or initials, usually stands for the owner of the model, while numbers tend to refer to the size or mould type, rather than the date. Symbols, such as stars or anchors, are often used as marks, and sometimes letters also indicate size and mould type.

Having found your mark, you can then look it up at your local library in the doll bible: Dorothy S., Elizabeth A. and Evelyn J. Coleman, *The Collector's Encyclopaedia of Dolls*, 2 vols (London, Robert Hale, 1968/86). This is an invaluable publication. Not only does it list the names of makers alphabetically, and explain different types of manufacture – bisque, wax, wood – but it also provides a wonderful guide to understanding your toy. For example, you can look up 'Age of Dolls' for advice on dating, or 'Bodies of Dolls' for information on composition. Leaf through the encyclopaedia for the information you need.

Original clothes are very important, and can greatly enhance the value of a doll. The seminal book on dolls' clothes is also written by the Colemans: *The Collector's Book of Dolls' Clothes*, London, Robert Hale, 1976.

Other recommended authors include Constance Eileen King, for books both on dolls and dolls' houses, and Caroline Goodfellow, *Understanding Dolls* (Woodbridge, Antique Collectors' Club, 1986).

Dangers to beware of include reproductions and dolls that have been altered or tampered with, as when the wrong head has been put on the wrong body. Obviously such knowledge only comes with experience, so if in doubt consult a specialist.

For up-to-date information about dealers, doll clubs, repairers, fairs, specialist museums and publications, a useful purchase is *The UK Doll Directory*, available from Hugglets (PO Box 290, Brighton BN2 1DR, Tel: 0273 697974) for £2.95 plus 50p postage.

Metal and Mechanical Toys

With the exception of very early models, many toys are likely to be marked in some way with either a monogram or a name, and the country of origin. Although you might be able to identify your toy from its mark, this will not necessarily tell you if it is valuable. As toy dealer P. McAskie explains: 'Condition is all important with toys, especially with modern examples where, if they are not mint, they do not sell. Toys are common as compared to other antiques, so the collector can afford to pick and choose.' To the outsider, this choice can appear to be based on the most esoteric criteria. Certain model cars, for example, are collected not just for their age or type, but for a particular shade of colour ('usually ugly', notes McAskie) that was used by a factory for only a couple of months, because they had run out of their usual paint. These accidents of fate are not the kind of information that gets recorded in a firm's catalogues, and the only way to gain such knowledge is to talk to dealers and collectors, and to study the subject in depth.

★

Because condition is so important, toy dealers and collectors have established their own vocabulary to describe the surface appearance of a toy. Terms vary a little but the basic system is as follows:

'Mint': perfect condition, as though it has just left the factory.
'Excellent': looks mint, but has some minor blemishes.
'Good': has been played with, but still in good condition.
'Fair': somewhat worn but still attractive enough to be collectable.
'Poor': from just below fair to a complete write-off.
The same terms are also applied to boxes.

TIN TOYS

Fawdry, Marguerite. *British Tin Toys*, London, New Cavendish Books, 1990

Pressland, David. *The Art of the Tin Toy*, London, New Cavendish Books, 1976

DIECAST TOYS

Cieslik, J. & M. *Lehmann Toys: The History of E. P. Lehmann, 1881–1981*, Levy, Allen (ed), London, New Cavendish Books, 1982

Cleemput, Marcel R. Van. *The Great Book of Corgi 1956–83*, London, New Cavendish Books, 1989

Matchbox. *Models of Yesteryear – The Collection* (this is a loose-leaf book designed to be added to as new models are produced)

Orr, Stewart A. and McGimpsey, Kevin W. *Collecting Matchbox Diecast Toys: First Forty Years*. Chester, Major Productions, 1989

Richardson, Mike and Sue. *Dinky Toys and Modelled Miniatures*, London, New Cavendish Books, 1981

Thompson, G. *Spot-On Diecast Models by Tri-ang*, Sparkford, 1983

Thompson, G. M. K. *British Diecasts: A Collectors' Guide to Toy Cars, Vans and Trucks*, Yeovil, G. T. Foulis & Co, 1980

Trench, Patrick. *Model Cars and Other Road Vehicles*, London, Pelham Books, 1983

Also look for publications by Dr Edward Force, John Ramsay and the Hornby Collectors Series.

TOY SOLDIERS AND FIGURINES

Garratt, John G. (ed). *The World Encyclopaedia of Model Soldiers*, London, Frederick Muller, 1981

Opie, James, *Britain's Toy Soldiers, 1893–1932*, London, Victor Gollancz, 1985
British Toy Soldiers, 1893 to the Present Day, London, Arms and Armour Press, 1985
Collecting Toy Soldiers, London, Collins Willow, 1987

TOY TRAINS

Foster, M. *Hornby Dublo Trains 1938–64*, London, 1980

Fuller, Roland. *The Bassett-Lowke Story*, Levy, Allen (ed), London, New Cavendish Books, 1982

Grave, Chris and Julie. *The Hornby Gauge 'O' System*, London, New Cavendish Books, 1985

Levy, Allen. *A Century of Model Trains*, London, New Cavendish Books, 1974

McCrindell, Ron. *Toy Trains*, Twickenham, Tiger Books International plc, 1989

Whitehouse, Patrick and Levy, Allen (eds). *The World of Model Trains*, London, Bison Books, 1978

Teddy Bears

The teddy bears most likely to be worth serious money are the Steiff bears, recognisable by the button in the left ear, or conversely by two little holes where the button has been removed. The most collectable are the early Steiff bears (1903–1910) with long limbs, felt pads, boot button eyes and humps – not a very attractive prospect to the non-aficionado. As one Portobello 'teddy specialist' advises, a tip for recognising early bears is to look for long arms and big feet, since early models were based on real bears and were designed to look as though they might stand on all fours; black button eyes are also a sign of age. Other makes apart from Steiff can also be collectable: Merrythought, Chad Valley, Bing,

Herman. Look out for the label, often to be found on one of the pads. The condition of the bear is very important, so check the fur and the pads; colour can also affect its value. There are a number of books on teddy bears and Pauline Cockrill's *The Ultimate Teddy Bear Book* (London, Dorling Kindersley, 1991) provides a marvellously clear pictorial account of teddy history and composition.

For specialist advice, *The UK Teddy Bear Guide*, published by Hugglets (see under dolls for details), will tell you everything you need to know about dealers, repairers, and collections. The British Teddy Bear Association hosts two annual teddy bear festivals, in London and Stratford, where you can take your bear along for a free identification and valuation.

Other recommended books include:

Axe, John. *The Magic of Merrythought*, Maryland, 1986
Cieslik, J. and M. *Button in Ear, the Teddy Bear and his Friends*, Verlag, 1989 (a book about Steiff which is particularly helpful for decoding buttons and labels and for dating the firm's products)
Hebbs, Pam. *Collecting Teddy Bears*, London, Collins, 1988
Schoonmaker, Patricia. *A Collector's History of the Teddy Bear*, Maryland, 1981

✍ III. EXPERT WITNESSES: MUSEUMS AND MISCELLANEOUS SOURCES

The collectables departments at the auction houses are a good place to take your toys to be identified and valued, as they cover every area and the staff are used to seeing a wide range of objects. For more specialist advice, try finding a dealer who concentrates in your particular subject. Curiously perhaps to the outsider, toy and doll dealers do not mix; each works separately in his or her own field. For a list of dealers, consult LAPADA (see page 14), specialist directories, and collector's magazines, and ask round for recommendations.

Britain's Museum of Childhood is in Bethnal Green, but many national museums have important holdings of toys, and there are a number of privately run toy museums that have excellent collections and often specialise in particular areas, such as Dinky Toys or Tri–ang. The latter are sometimes interested in purchasing toys, so if you are considering selling your item, it might be a good idea to get an independent valuation before approaching them.

If the firm that produced your toy is still in operation you can try contacting them for further information. Even if they cannot help you themselves, they should be able to put you in contact with a relevant expert or society. For example, for publications and general information about Matchbox toys, contact the Consumer Service Department, Matchbox Toys Ltd, Unit 1A, Swift Park Industrial Estate, Old Leicester Road, Rugby, Warwickshire CV21 1DZ.

Matchbox also has an International Collectors Association (MICA) that was founded in 1985. Members receive a magazine that covers all aspects of collecting Matchbox toys, both old and new. You can write to them at 13a Lower Bridge Street, Chester CH1 1RS.

The toy field abounds in collectors' clubs: some concentrate on a particular type of toy such as the British Toy Soldier Society, while others such as the Corgi Collector Club, specialise in individual factories.

As with all other antique societies, these institutions offer a chance to meet specialists and to share information and enthusiasm; their journals and publications can also provide a rich source of knowledge. The addresses for these societies can be found in related magazines and directories, but toy museums and dealers should also be able to help.

🏛 MUSEUMS

London

Bethnal Green Museum of Childhood

Britain's national Museum of Childhood houses the largest public collection of toys in the world, including dolls and dolls' houses; games and toys of every sort; children's books, children's clothes, and nursery furniture. The museum is happy to help people with their research, but resources are limited, so always make an appointment before bringing in an item. The museum's library of historic children's books (the Renier Collection) is open to researchers by appointment only.

London Toy and Model Museum

The museum houses more than 5,000 trains, planes, boats, dolls, animals, and bears. Consultations are available by appointment.

Pollock's Toy Museum

The collection includes dolls, puppets, toy theatres, and games. The museum specialises in folk and popular toys. Consultations are available by appointment.

Regional

Bantock House Museum, Wolverhampton

The museum contains a collection of dolls and toys.

The Chester Toy and Doll Museum

This privately-run museum houses a wide selection of toys, including dolls, an important Dinky and Meccano display, and the largest collection of Matchbox toys on public view worldwide. The museum holds a comprehensive archive relating to Lesney products and Matchbox toys, including documents, cuttings and catalogues; it is also home to the Matchbox International Collectors Association (MICA). Consultations are given on Saturday mornings and by post, but a self-addressed, stamped envelope is requested.

Judges' Lodgings, Lancaster

The museum houses a collection of toys, dolls and games. Consultations are available by appointment.

National Railway Museum, York

The museum covers the history of the railway in Britain in all its various forms. The museum holds an important collection of model trains. There is a major archive and reference collection, which includes printed books, periodicals, timetables, photographs, posters, paintings and pictorial material, and a sound archive. The Reading Room is open Mon–Fri: 10.30–5, but make an appointment before you visit. Enquiries are answered by appointment and by post.

Ribchester Museum of Childhood

This privately run museum holds a large collection of dolls' houses, dolls' house miniatures, and general toys, including a wide range of Tri-ang. It also boasts the only collection of its kind of 'Flea-Circus' material and memorabilia. The museum's library is open by request only, and identifications are made by appointment.

Warwick Doll Museum

The museum houses a large collection of dolls, from 1800 onwards, as well as games, toys, automata, and children's books. Consultations are available by appointment.

17

Arms, Armour and Related Material

✍ I. EXAMINE THE EVIDENCE

Begin by examining your object carefully – and I mean carefully! 'A weapon is an enemy even to its owner', claims one Turkish proverb, so assume that all guns are loaded until it is proved otherwise, and make sure that powder and shot flasks are empty. 'Empty any gunpowder down the loo,' advises arms and armour dealer Michael German. Treat all weapons with respect and circumspection.

Whatever your item is, be it a musket or helmet, submit it to the usual process of examination (see Part One). Look over it closely, measure it, photograph it and collate any information about a known provenance. Examine its shape, construction and decoration, and transcribe, photograph or take rubbings of any marks. These could include maker's or retailer's marks, town marks, owner's monograms, arsenal stamps, coats of arms, regimental symbols and proof marks. The latter show that the efficiency of the object has been tested, or proved, by an official body, and are found, for example, on English gun barrels, where they should not be confused with silver hallmarks, as sometimes happens. Even if you do not understand what individual stamps refer to, note them down, maintaining an open mind, since it is possible for the art criminal to engrave metalwork with a prestigious coat of arms, or an inscription, that bears no relation to the object's history.

In the field of arms and armour, the art detective should beware of reproductions, both modern and nineteenth century. The latter are now extremely collectable in their own right, and were often made to decorate Victorian baronial halls and gothic mansions. The main feature that distinguishes copies from originals is that they were not generally intended to be used, and this provides a helpful clue for identification. Handle the item to see how it feels and works. 'With armour, see if it looks as though it would fit on somebody,' advises Sarah Barter Bailey, Librarian at the Royal Armouries. 'Could it be worn by a human being? Are the eye sockets in the right place? Do the joints work properly? Is it practical?' Whatever your object is, imagine using it. Does it feel comfortable and well balanced and could it, in your opinion, fulfil its apparent function? (N.B. Any waving around of swords or guns is best carried out with care and in private, unless you want to be laughed at, injured or arrested.)

✍ II. THE INVESTIGATION

📖 LIBRARY RESEARCH AND BASIC REFERENCE BOOKS

The books listed below, available from major libraries, will help you with the initial identification of objects, makers, or marks, and with background information. Forewarned is forearmed, so, if possible, it is a good idea to do some preliminary research, particularly the checking of makers' names, before consulting a specialist.

Bibliography

Bailey, De Witt and Nie, Douglas A. *English Gunmakers: The Birmingham and Provincial Gun Trade in the 18th and 19th Century*, London, Arms & Armour Press, 1978

Blackmore, Howard L. *British Military Firearms 1650–1850*, London, Herbert Jenkins, 1961

A Dictionary of London Gunmakers 1350–1850, London, Phaidon Christie's, 1986

Guns and Rifles of the World, London, Batsford, 1965

Blair, Claude. *European and American Arms*, London, Batsford, 1962

European Armour c. 1066 to c. 1700, London, Batsford, 1958

Blair, Claude (ed). *Pistols of the World*, London, Batsford, 1968

Pollard's History of Firearms, London, Newnes Books, 1983

Blair, Claude, and Tarassuk, Leonid (eds). *The Complete Encyclopaedia of Arms and Weapons*, London, Batsford, 1982

Byron, David. *The Official Guide to Gunmarks*, Powys, The Border Press, 1990

Carey, A. Merwyn. *English, Irish and Scottish Firearm Makers*, London, Arms & Armour Press, 1967

Hawkins, Peter. *The Price Guide to Antique Guns and Pistols*, Woodbridge, Antique Collectors' Club, 1973

Laking, Sir G. F. *A Record of European Arms and Armour through Seven Centuries*, G. Bell & Sons, 1920–2

Southwick, Leslie. *The Price Guide to Antique Edged Weapons*, Woodbridge, Antique Collectors' Guide, 1982

Stone, G. C. *A Glossary of the Construction, Decoration and Use of Arms and Armor*, New York, 1961

Whitelaw, Charles E. *Scottish Arms Makers: A Biographical Dictionary of Makers of Firearms, Edged Weapons and Armour Working in Scotland from the 14th Century to 1870*, London, Arms & Armour Press, 1977

📖 **FURTHER ENQUIRIES AND SPECIALIST LIBRARIES**

The specialist museums listed on pages 176–7 house major libraries related to their field. For general historical and archival research, refer to Part One.

The Public Record Office, London (see page 53), could, in certain circumstances, be a useful centre of investigation. Its various holdings include the records of the Board of Ordnance who, between 1683 and 1855, were responsible for the supply of arms and equipment to the British Army and Navy. The Tower of London displays many such weapons, distinctively marked with the letters 'BO' under a broad arrow, signifying government ownership. Remember that the Ordnance Records are likely to be extremely general. The PRO also keeps material concerning registration marks (see page 54), which you might come across on some items.

Patent Office records could also be helpful if, for instance, you are researching a gun patented in the nineteenth century and want to go back to the original designs and specifications.

✍ III. Expert Witnesses: Museums and Miscellaneous Sources

The most famous collection of arms and armour in Britain, and a good place to begin your investigations, is the Royal Armouries at the Tower of London. If your object is specifically connected with any branch of the armed forces, contact their main museum for information. Some regiments have their own museums or collections, and the National Army Museum should be able to point you in the right direction.

As with every other subject, advice and valuations can be sought from the major auction houses – Christie's is particularly recommended – and dealers – consult BADA and LAPADA.

🏛 SPECIALIST MUSEUMS IN LONDON

Imperial War Museum

This is the place to go with twentieth-century material since the theme of the museum is all conflicts involving Britain in the twentieth century, and the two World Wars in particular. The extensive reference library is open to the public by appointment, as is the photographic library and the department of documents, sound records and film. Consultations are available by appointment or by post.

National Army Museum

The museum covers the history of the armies of Britain, the Empire and the Commonwealth, from the foundation of the Yeoman of the Guard by Henry VIII in 1485 to the present day. It is home to one of the largest collections of military costumes in the world and has an extensive display of weapons. The Reading Room (Tues–Sat: 10–4.30) is open to holders of readers' tickets, which may be obtained by written application to the Director. The library contains over 30,000 books, as well as the letters, journals and papers of military figures both major and minor. There is a large collection of prints, drawings and photographs. Consultation and identifications are available by appointment and by post.

National Maritime Museum

The museum has a magnificent library and is the place for all your enquiries about naval weapons and related material.

Royal Air Force Museum

Britain's national museum of aviation covers the story of flight and the history of the Royal Air Force. As well as aeroplanes, instruments, armaments, uniforms, and memorabilia, the museum also holds an interesting collection of related portraits, drawings and sculptures. Consultations are available by appointment with the appropriate department or by post. According to the major librarian, among the more frequent enquiries they receive is the request to identify wooden plane propellers, now extremely collectable, and identifiable if you have the correct serial numbers. The library, which includes much archival material, is open Monday to Friday, 10–5, by appointment.

The Royal Armouries, HM Tower of London

The Royal Armouries is the national museum of arms and armour, and the oldest public museum in Britain. The collection, one of the most important in the world, includes both European and Oriental material. Curatorial staff will give opinions on objects, by appointment, Mon–Sat: 10–12; 2–4.

The library contains over 10,000 books, pamphlets, periodicals and manuscripts from around the world on the history of arms and armour and the Tower of London. Among its many useful treasures is a massive card index of marks of every type found on arms or armour, which is extremely helpful both for identifications and comparisons. The library

is open to the genuine researcher by appointment, Mon–Fri:
10–12; 2–5. Other services provided by the Armouries include
advice on conservation and a technical analysis of objects (for
which a charge is made).

🏛 **MUSEUMS GENERAL**

London

The Victoria & Albert Museum

The museum has a collection of European and Oriental arms
and armour. Consultations are available at the Metalwork
Department on Tuesday afternoons, 2.30–4.30.

The Wallace Collection

The collection includes European and Oriental arms and
armour. Consultations are available by appointment.

Regional

Fitzwilliam Museum, Cambridge

The museum houses a collection of European and Oriental
arms and armour. Consultations are available by appointment.

Manchester Museum

The Simon Archery Collection consists of archery material
from all over the world and includes some 2,000 exhibits.
The Simon Archery Library has a comprehensive collection
of books and periodicals dating from 1792 to the present day.
Consultations and viewings are available by appointment.

Scotland

Glasgow Art Gallery and Museum

The European arms and armour collection also includes many
Scottish weapons and firearms. Consultations are available by
appointment.

Royal Museum of Scotland, Edinburgh

The museum includes a collection of European and Oriental
arms and armour, and Highland weaponry. Consultations are
available by appointment.

✉ **USEFUL ADDRESSES**

The Armourers' Company and the Worshipful Company of Gunmakers might be able to help with information and advice. The records of both these institutions are held by the Guildhall Library in London.

Armourers and Brasiers' Company
Armourers Hall
81 Coleman Street
London EC2R 5BJ
Tel: 071 606 1199

The Worshipful Company of Gunmakers
48 Commercial Road
London E1 1LP
Tel: 071 481 2695

The latter is home to the London Gun Barrel Proof House and is a good place for information about London gunmakers.

Apart from London, the other major gunmaking town in Britain was Birmingham, where guns are also proved. For further information contact:

Birmingham Gun Barrel Proof House
Banbury Street
Birmingham B5 5RH
Tel: 021 643 386

✉ **EXISTING COMPANIES**

Some famous and long-established gunmakers have preserved their archives and should you be fortunate enough to own one of their pieces, they should be able to assist you with your enquiries.

Holland & Holland Ltd, Gunmakers (est 1835), 31 Bruton Street, London W1X 7DD, Tel: 071 499 4411, keep records from the beginning of the firm's history, and will offer help with identification and valuation. 'We receive about fifty enquiries a week,' said the man in charge of the gun room, sounding understandably exhausted, when I phoned them up, 'but we are always ready to help.'

James Purdey and Sons, Gun and Rifle Makers (est 1814), 57 South Audley Street, London W1Y 6ED, Tel: 071 499 1801, maintain records of every piece they have ever produced and also provide assistance with valuations and identifications, as do Boss & Co Ltd, Gunmakers (est 1812), 13 Dover Street, London W1X 3PH, Tel: 071 493 0711/1127.

✉ **SOCIETIES**

The Arms and Armour Society
The Royal Armouries, HM Tower of London

The Historical Breechloading Small Arms Association
Imperial War Museum

Re-enactment groups — those societies occupying themselves with staging reproduction battles complete in everything except the blood and guts — carry out much serious archival research in order to recreate their arms and armour accurately, and could conceivably be a source of some assistance.

18
Oriental and Islamic Works

This is a subject where the beginner should tread as though walking on 100-year-old eggshells. Oriental ceramics and works of art are an extremely specialised area. According to Bluetts, a respected dealer in the field, the market is flooded with fakes, forgeries and genuine period reproductions. For example, an eighteenth-century Chinese craftsman would in all honesty copy a twelfth-century piece in respectful tribute to its creator. The same patterns and techniques have been followed throughout the centuries; years of knowledge are required to identify items, and even experts frequently disagree about the interpretation of a particular work. 'All too often, there is no such thing as a final answer,' notes Roger Bluett gloomily. In this field, therefore, the art detective's best solution is to seek professional advice before embarking upon serious library investigations (see Part One).

✍ I. EXAMINE THE OBJECT

Examine your object, note down measurements and relevant details, transcribe any provenance information and take photographs. 'The more, the better,' urges Catherine Harvey from the British Museum's Oriental Students' Room. 'Take pictures of any particularly interesting features, any marks, any calligraphy, and please, please, make them as clear as possible.'

II. THE INVESTIGATION

LIBRARY RESEARCH

The field covered by this section is extremely wide. It would be impossible to provide a bibliography to suit every specialised need, so I have confined myself to suggesting a handful of standard works, readily available at any local library. These will supply background information and suggest further and more specific sources of reference. Museums, specialist dealers and bookshops (see page 41) should also be able to help with reading lists.

Bibliography

Ettinghausen, Richard. *The Art and Architecture of Islam*, Pelican History of Art, London, Penguin, 1987

Frankfort, Henri. *The Art and Architecture of the Ancient Orient*, Pelican History of Art, London, Penguin, 1970

Paine, Robert Treat and Soper, Alexander. *The Art and Architecture of Japan*, Pelican History of Art, London, Penguin, 1971

Rowland, Benjamin. *The Art and Architecture of India*, Pelican History of Art, London, Penguin, 1977

Sickman, L. and Soper, Alexander. *The Art and Architecture of China,* Pelican History of Art, London, Penguin, 1971

Relevant libraries include:

Oriental and India Office Collections
The British Library
197 Blackfriars Road
London SE1 8NG
Tel: 071 412 7873
Mon–Fri: 9.30–5.45; Sat: 9.30–12.45
Prints & Drawings: Mon–Fri: 2.30–5, by appointment only

The India Office part of the library concentrates on India

from the Raj period up to Independence (1947), on the East India Company and on South Asia. As well as printed material, the library houses some 28,000 Oriental manuscripts; archives held include those of the East India Company, the India Office, and the private papers of many individuals who worked and travelled in India. The Prints and Drawings Section has an unrivalled collection of drawings by British artists in India and the East, works by Indian artists, Persian and Indian miniatures, and a unique archive of photographs dating from the nineteenth century and recording daily life in India, architectural subjects, etc. The Oriental holdings, formerly housed in a separate building, include a comprehensive collection of Oriental material in the languages of Asia and North-East Africa (contact the collection for further details). Opinions are given on manuscript material, miniatures, and related fields, by appointment only.

A British Library card is required to use the collections, and for specific enquiries, the library recommends writing rather than telephoning, since the letter can then be sent to the relevant specialist.

Royal Asiatic Society Library
60 Queens Gardens
London W2 3AF
Tel: 071 724 4741
Mon, Wed, Thurs: 10–5; Fri: 10–8.30

The library is open to non-society members by appointment only, and includes material pertaining to South-East Asia and Ethiopia. There is a significant, if somewhat uneven, collection of publications connected with Asiatic art. The society also holds a collection of over 2,000 prints, drawings and paintings of Oriental interest, which includes Indian Mogul material, works by European artists in India and native Indian artists working in the European style, topographical studies, Chinese and Japanese works.

School of Oriental and African Studies
University of London
Malet Street
London WC1E 7HP

Tel: 071 637 2388
Term time: Mon–Thurs: 9–8.45; Fri: 9–7; Sat: 9.30–5
Summer: Mon–Fri: 9–5; Sat: 9.30–5

Part of London University, the library holds material relating to Africa and the Near, Middle and Far East, and includes a comprehensive art section. The library is open to non-university members by written appointment. A letter of recommendation is necessary.

✍ III. EXPERT WITNESSES: MUSEUMS AND SPECIALIST ADVICE

Take the object itself, or if that is not possible, your selection of photographs and details, to an expert witness. If your local museum cannot help you, then try one of the museums listed below. In London, the British Museum and the V&A are good places to begin your enquiries. For valuations and advice in the commercial sector consult:

Spink and Sons Ltd
5–7 King Street
London SW1Y 6QS
Tel: 071 930 7888
Mon–Fri: 9.30–5.30

Areas of speciality include Chinese, Japanese, Indian, South-East Asian and Islamic Art. On-the-spot verbal advice and valuations are given free of charge, but there is a fee for written valuations.

Also try the major auction houses and relevant recommended dealers.

🏛 MUSEUMS

London

Percival David Foundation of Chinese Art
Part of the School of Oriental and African Studies, the

foundation houses a unique collection of Chinese ceramics and a library of East Asian and Western books dealing with Chinese art and culture. The library is open to the public by written appointment, Mon–Fri: 10.30–1, 2–4.45. Consultations are available by appointment and by post, and individual objects may be left at the museum for assessment.

The British Museum
The Students' Room
Department of Oriental Antiquities

The Oriental Department provides an opinion service Mon–Fri: 2.15–4; the Western Asiatic Department, Mon–Fri: 2–4.30. Though there is always a member of staff on duty, if you already have some idea about what your piece is, be it a Chinese pot or an Indian bronze, phone beforehand to ensure that the appropriate curator will be there to answer your questions. The museum can help with identifications, general research and will also supply bibliographies. An appointment must be made in order to consult the Japanese Department.

The Victoria & Albert Museum

The V&A houses primary displays of Indian, Near Eastern and Far Eastern art in all its forms. Its textile and ceramic study collections include large groups of Chinese, Japanese and Persian material. The impressive number of objects on view makes the V&A an excellent place to compare and contrast your object, and to learn about your chosen subject in general. Each department offers an opinion service on Tuesday afternoons, 2–4.30, but make sure you phone up beforehand to check which department and expert can best assist you in your enquiries.

Regional

Ashmolean Museum, Oxford

The Eastern Art Department houses antiquities from China, Japan, the Indian subcontinent and Islamic cultures of the Near East. The collection is particularly strong in Chinese and Japanese ceramics. Archives include the Cresswell Archive of Islamic Architecture. Consultations are available by appointment.

Fitzwilliam Museum, Cambridge

The collection includes Middle Eastern antiquities, Oriental porcelains, bronzes, hardstones, lacquers, arms and armour, Japanese drawings, etc. Consultations are available by appointment.

Oriental Museum, Durham

The museum specialises in Oriental art, and concentrates on works from China; it also holds an important collection of Egyptian antiquities. Consultations are available by appointment and by post.

Republic of Ireland

Chester Beatty Library and Gallery of Oriental Art, Dublin

The Chester Beatty holds an internationally important collection of Islamic, Chinese, Japanese, Persian, Turkish and Indian books and artefacts, and biblical papyri and manuscripts ranging from the thirteenth to nineteenth centuries. There is a major holding of Japanese prints, and the museum houses the world's largest collection of Chinese jade books and rhinoceros horn cups. The library is open to the serious researcher by application; a recommendation is required. Consultations and opinions are available by appointment.

Scotland

Royal Museum of Scotland, Edinburgh

Oriental material in the collection includes ceramics, glass, metalwork, arms and armour, ivories, jade, costumes and textiles from the Near, Middle and Far East; there is also an important collection of Hindu and Buddhist sculpture. Consultations are available by appointment – preferably requested in writing – with the appropriate curator. The museum's library is open to members of the public with serious and specific enquiries, by appointment only.

✉ **SPECIALIST SOCIETY**
The Oriental Ceramic Society
31b Torrington Square
London WC1E 7JL
Tel: 071 636 7985

The society is concerned with all aspects of Chinese art.

19
Archaeology and Anthropology: Antiquities and Ethnographic Material

As far as the art detective is concerned, what unites the material included in this chapter is its difficulty. Whether you are researching a Roman artefact or an African drum, they offer no easy clues to the amateur sleuth in the form of nice little labels or easily recognisable signatures. Unless you already have a good idea of what you are looking at, do not waste time at the library, but go straight to an expert. Try your local museum or, if they cannot help you, contact one of the institutions listed below. There the relevant specialist will be able to assess your object and, if necessary, point you in the right direction for any library and archive investigation (also see Part One).

✍ I. EXAMINE THE EVIDENCE

Examine the object, record provenance details, take measurements and photographs.

⚐ II. EXPERT WITNESSES: MUSEUMS AND MISCELLANEOUS SOURCES

Archaeology and anthropology go together like Holmes and Watson, and many of the museums listed below deal in both fields. The following is only a short selection. For a comprehensive list of ethnographic and anthropological collections in Britain, consult the *Museum Ethnographers' Group Survey of Ethnographic Collections in the United Kingdom, Eire and the Channel Islands*, ed Yvonne Schumann, 1986, and for further information generally, see the museum directories listed in chapter 2.

For valuations and identifications, go to a good dealer or an auction house: Christie's is particularly recommended in this field.

🏛 MUSEUMS

London

The British Museum

The vastness of the museum's archaeological collection is matched by the broad range of experts available for consultation. The following departments all offer an opinion service, Mon–Fri: 2–4.30: Egyptian; Greek and Roman; Prehistoric and Romano-British; Medieval and later. Although there is always a curator on duty, it is a good idea to ring beforehand if you wish to speak to a specialist in any particular field.

Horniman Museum and Library

The museum houses ethnographical collections from all parts of the world, including a major holding of musical instruments. Consultations are available by appointment. The museum's library, specialising in subjects covered by the collections, is open to the public Tues–Sat: 10.30–5.45; Sun: 2–5.45.

Museum of Mankind

The museum's collections come from the indigenous peoples of Africa, Australia, the Pacific, North and South America, and from certain parts of Asia and Europe. The museum covers both ancient and contemporary cultures and noteworthy exhibits include large collections of Benin bronzes, Eskimo art, African sculpture, and textiles. The museum has one of the best anthropological libraries in the world, and applications for a reader's ticket are available from the information desk. Research enquiries are dealt with in the Students' Room, Mon–Sat: 1–4.45, where objects may be taken for identification.

Regional

Ashmolean Museum, Oxford

The museum's antiquities collection covers the art and archaeology of Europe, the Mediterranean world and the Near East from the earliest times until the Middle Ages. There is an important cast gallery of classical sculpture, and archives include the Bearly Archive of photographs of Greek vases. Consultations are available by appointment.

Birmingham City Museum and Art Gallery

The museum's comprehensive archaeology collection includes material from Greece, Rome, the Middle and Near East, Central and Southern America. Consultations are available by appointment.

Brighton Museum and Art Gallery

The museum houses an important ethnographic collection. Consultations are available by appointment.

City of Bristol Museum and Art Gallery

The museum has archaeological and ethnographic collections. Consultations are available by appointment.

Cambridge University Museum of Archaeology and Anthropology

The museum's major archaeological and anthropological collections are particularly rich in material from the Stone Age, Bronze Age, Roman and Anglo-Saxon periods. Objects may be left at the museum for identification.

Fitzwilliam Museum, Cambridge

Egyptian, Greek, Roman and Middle Eastern antiquities are included in the museum's collections. Consultations are available by appointment.

Liverpool Museum

The museum's important antiquities collection includes Etruscan jewellery, Anglo-Saxon remains, Roman works and medieval ivories. It also has an ethnographic collection. Consultations are available by appointment.

The Manchester Museum

The museum's major display of archaeological material includes one of the finest Egyptian collections in Britain. Research projects based at the museum include the Egyptian Mummy Research project and the resulting International Mummy Data Base, which receives and stores information about mummies from institutions around the world. There is also an important ethnographic collection. Identifications can be made by appointment or objects may be left at the museum for assessment.

Pitt-Rivers Museum, Oxford

The museum specialises in ethnography and archaeology worldwide, and the holdings include a musical instrument collection (mainly ethnographic) that is one of the largest in existence. The Balfour Library is open to the public (telephone for opening times) and the archives, mainly anthropological, may be viewed by arrangement. Consultations are available by appointment.

Republic of Ireland

National Museum of Ireland, Dublin

The museum houses a major collection of antiquities that includes gold personal ornaments from the Bronze Age and Early Christian metalwork. The library and archives are open by special request; consultations are available by appointment and by post.

Scotland

Glasgow Art Gallery and Museum

The museum contains some archaeological and ethnographic material. Consultations are available by appointment.

Hunterian Museum, Glasgow

The museum houses major archaeological and anthropological collections. Consultations are available by appointment.

Royal Museum of Scotland, Edinburgh

The Royal Museum's treasures include antiquities from Greece, Rome and the Ancient Near East; an important Ancient Egyptian collection; Scottish material of major importance; and an ethnographic collection. Consultations are available by appointment.

20

Antique Mechanical and Domestic Appliances

In these days when almost anything seems to be collectable, there is a small but growing market for antique mechanical and domestic appliances. A number of museums have mechanical/domestic collections. According to Christie's expert Christopher Proudfoot, who collects ancient lawnmowers, sewing machines and typewriters are now well-established in the auction rooms, with rare models fetching thousands of pounds. Many dealers specialise in 'Kitchenalia', a horrible word that sounds like a housewife going mad with a breadknife, and even the humble vacuum cleaner has its enthusiasts.

Obviously most of the obsolete domestic machinery that you are likely to come across in your attic or on flea market stalls will not be of any great value or historical interest. Serious collectors of sewing machines, typewriters, and so on crave the rare models. 'We don't want the famous brand names such as Singer,' explains Maggie Snell of the International Sewing Machine Collectors' Society (ISMACS). 'We want the stuff that wasn't successful, made by the little guy in the workshop at the bottom of his garden who sold nothing and then went bust.'

Ironically, given the practical nature of the subject, as far as the marketplace is concerned, the condition of the surface appearance is far more important than functioning mechanics. 'I don't give a damn if a machine is in perfect working order,' says Proudfoot. 'Visual appeal and/or innate rarity are what sells.'

For the art detective, this field can prove surprisingly fascinating. Not only are many of the objects interesting in their own right, but in investigating their history, you are tracking down the ancestors of today's mechanical and domestic appliances, so commonplace in our modern homes that most of us never give them a thought. While exploring the past, you learn about the present – one of the great satisfactions of research.

✍ I. EXAMINE THE EVIDENCE

Examine the object, take photographs – the item could well be too big to lug about with you – and record provenance information. As you are likely to be dealing with a product rather than an artefact, look for a brand name and note down any numbers and inscribed information. Refer to Part One for more general information about conducting your investigation.

✍ II. THE INVESTIGATION

📖 LIBRARY RESEARCH AND BASIC REFERENCE BOOKS

In comparison with other more traditional collectables, there are few books devoted to the field of mechanical domestic appliances. A short bibliography is listed below. Auction catalogues can be a useful source of reference, and collectables guides will often contain some basic information about household 'antiques'.

If you want to go into your particular subject in any depth, you might well find that you have to carry out your own research using such sources as contemporary periodicals, commercial catalogues, and publications connected with the major industrial exhibitions of the period. In certain circumstances, it could even be useful to trace the original patent (see page

53). Scientific libraries are a good place to conduct your investigations (see chapter 14), as are institutions connected with design and industry.

If the firm that made your object is still in operation, they might have preserved some background information or an archival collection, so you could try contacting them for further suggestions.

Bibliography

GENERAL

Hardyment, Christina. *From Mangle to Microwave: Mechanization of the Household*, Cambridge, Polity Press, 1988

Miller, Muriel M. *Household Treasures*, London, Guinness Publishing, 1990

Pearsall, Ronald. *Collecting Mechanical Antiques*, Newton Abbot, David & Charles, 1973

SEWING MACHINES

Cooper, Grace Rogers. *The Sewing Machine: Its Invention and Development*, Washington, Smithsonian Institution Press, 1976

Godfrey, Frank P. *An International History of the Sewing Machine*, London, Robert Hale, 1982

Head, Carol. *Old Sewing Machines*, Aylesbury, Shire Publications, 1982

Jewell, B. F. *Veteran Sewing Machines*, Newton Abbot, David & Charles, 1975

TYPEWRITERS

Beecher, W. A. *Century of the Typewriter*, London Heinemann, 1974

Delgado, A. *The Enormous File: Social History of the Office*, London, John Murray, 1979

✍ III. EXPERT WITNESSES: MUSEUMS AND MISCELLANEOUS SOURCES

Many museums, in particular science, industrial and local history museums, will include mechanical and domestic collections, particularly if the firm that produced them, or the industry itself, was somehow relevant to their area. The libraries at both the Science and the Design Museums should provide a good source of further reference.

Advice, identifications and valuations can be sought from auction houses and dealers, and LAPADA can supply details of shops with an interest in domestic antiques and other related subjects. Many specialists in the field, however, tend to operate from stalls in flea markets, somewhat out of the sphere of official organisations.

🏛 MUSEUMS

London

The Design Museum

The museum specialises in domestic and industrial design generally, but concentrates on the twentieth century. The museum's library (Tues–Sat: 11.30–6.30) is a good source of research and reference.

National Museum of Science and Industry

The Science Museum houses a magnificent collection of mechanical and domestic appliances, including Britain's national collection of typewriters (mostly in storage), and a fascinating display of household material ranging from carpet-sweepers to waterclosets, from the earliest models onwards. Consultations are available by appointment, and the library is open to the public.

Regional

Clydebank District Museum

When Singer's Clydebank factory closed down in 1980, the local museum inherited its archive collection of sewing machines, including not only the first Singers, but also machines produced by their competitors, as well as papers, parts, etc. It has the best public display of sewing machines in Britain, and features a valuable research centre. Consultations are available by appointment.

21

Musical Instruments: Classical and Rock

Sherlock Holmes doubtless knew every detail about the provenance of his famous violin, but how should the amateur detective approach the investigation of a musical instrument?

Classical and Instruments General

✍ I. EXAMINE THE EVIDENCE

Begin by examining the instrument and noting down any inscribed information. Do be sceptical, however, for according to violin specialist Charles Beare, many inferior nineteenth-century violins are dignified by the addition of a Stradivari label. 'Believing the label is the easiest way to waste time and money,' he warns.

Collate provenance details and be sure to keep together any relevant papers: a bill of sale, the retailer's guarantee, or any written information which could prove important (see Part One).

✍ II. THE INVESTIGATION

📖 LIBRARY RESEARCH AND BASIC REFERENCE BOOKS

A short bibliography of useful books is listed below. While these can tell you about the supposed maker of your instrument, only an expert can advise you if it is a fake, a commonplace object or a musical masterpiece.

Jeremy Montague, Curator of the Bate Collection, told how one afternoon a member of the public brought in a recorder purchased that morning for £4.10s from an Oxford market stall. He immediately recognised it to be a rare example by a famous baroque maker worth several thousand pounds. So do not spend too long in the library, but seek advice as soon as possible. Even if a specialist cannot give you such a satisfying answer as this, he or she will certainly save you time and effort.

Bibliography

Baines, A. *European and American Musical Instruments*, London, Batsford, 1966
   Woodwind Instruments and Their History, London, Faber & Faber, 1967
Boalch, D. M. *Makers of the Harpsichord and Clavichord 1440–1840*, Oxford, Clarendon Press, 1974
Hammer, W. *Master Italian Violinmakers*, Munich, 1976
Harding, Rosamond E. M. *The Piano-Forte: Its History Traced to the Great Exhibition of 1851* (1933), Woking, Surrey, Gresham Books, 1978
Henley, W. *Universal Dictionary of Violin and Bow Makers*, Brighton, 1959
Jalovec, Karel. *Encyclopaedia of Violin Makers*, London, Paul Hamlyn, 1968
Langwill, Lyndesay G. *An Index of Musical Wind-instrument Makers*, Edinburgh, L. G. Langwill, 1980
Sadie, Stanley (ed). *New Grove Dictionary of Musical Instruments*, London, 1984

✍ III. EXPERT WITNESSES: MUSEUMS AND MISCELLANEOUS SOURCES

Though many museums in Britain house musical collections, very few have curators who are also musicologists and have concentrated on the study of musical instruments. For general advice, the best museums to consult include the Horniman, the Bate Collection, Pitt-Rivers, and Edinburgh University Collection. It is always a good idea to phone the museum beforehand to see if it specialises in your particular type of instrument. Some collections will be better for woodwinds, others for keyboard instruments, and still others for ethnographic pieces. Even if museum staff can not help you themselves, they should be able to recommend someone who can.

For further information about relevant museums see Clifford Bevan, *Musical Instrument Collections in the British Isles*, (Winchester, Piccolo Press, 1990), an exhaustive and well-researched guide.

For advice and valuations, contact the major auction houses and specialist dealers through BADA and LAPADA.

🏛 MUSEUMS

London

British Museum

The British Museum holds the largest collection of musical instruments in Britain; several thousand pieces are distributed round the various departments of antiquities. It is the place to go for Mesopotamian harps, Roman cornua, Ancient Greek panpipes and Roman Egyptian crotals (not an anagram, but a bell or rattle), and early instruments in general. Instruments come from all over the world, and date from the Stone Age to the fourteenth century. Consultations are available by appointment with the relevant department.

Horniman Museum and Library

The Horniman has one of the major collections of musical instruments in the world – some 6,000 objects – encompassing pieces from every age and every culture. 'If ever anyone has tried to make a noise with it, we want one!' explains Frances Palmer, Keeper of Musical Instruments. With this policy in mind, the museum is one of the few, if not the only, British museum to have started to collect rock instruments. Consultations on most forms of musical instruments, particularly ethnographic, are available by appointment. The museum's library (closed Mondays) specialises in 'ethnomusicology'.

Museum of Mankind

The Museum of Mankind has one of the world's greatest ethnographic collections, which includes musical instruments from Africa, Asia, America, Europe, Australia and the Pacific. Works that are not displayed in exhibitions are stored, but may be viewed by appointment. Like the Horniman, this is a good place to go for the identification of ethnographic instruments. Contact the museum's Students' Room for details.

Royal College of Music

The Royal College has a stunning display of instruments that includes such treasures as the earliest surviving stringed keyboard in the world, a German clavytherium *circa* 1480, a spinet said to have belonged to Handel, a Stradivari violin, and guitars dating from the sixteenth century. As you pass through the college, you may have the chance to hear full orchestras in practice – a very uplifting experience on a cold winter's afternoon. Though the museum does not have sufficient staff to help with identifications, the college library is open to the general public for reference only, and is a useful place for research.

The Victoria & Albert Museum

As you might expect from Britain's national applied arts museum, the V&A has always collected instruments for their decorative rather than their musical qualities: a sixteenth-century spinet encrusted with semi-precious stones, instruments with cases designed by well-known artists and architects. This could be a useful place for researching the outside rather than the inner workings of your instrument. Contact the Furniture and Woodwork Department for advice.

Regional

The Bate Collection of Historical Instruments, Oxford

This is one of the few collections where instruments can be handled and played by serious students. The collection numbers over 1,000 pieces and includes woodwind, brass, harpsichords, clavichords and percussion instruments, from the baroque period to the present day. Identifications can be made by appointment.

Boosey and Hawkes Museum, Middlesex

A visit to the museum forms part of a guided tour of the Boosey and Hawkes factory, where you can see the manufacturing process of brass instruments and flutes from the raw materials stage right through to the final spit and polish. The museum houses one of the most important displays of brass and woodwind instruments in the country, with examples dating back to the seventeenth century.

Brighton Museum and Art Gallery

Brighton has a large display of both Western and ethnographic instruments, which includes such esoteric joys as the M. Willins Collection of Whistles, and instruments by Adolphe Sax.

Concertina Museum Collection, Belper

This private collection of concertinas is open to the public by appointment.

The Museum of Victorian Reed Organs, Saltaire, Shipley

The only museum in Europe devoted to reed organs: it houses some fifty instruments, in Victorian settings, and has much background material. Clearly this is the place to go if you are interested in researching reed organs.

The Musical Museum, Brentford

The museum holds a remarkable collection of keyboard and mechanical instruments, including pianolas, reproducing pianos and orchestrions.

Pitt-Rivers Museum, Oxford

A major collection of mainly ethnographic instruments, it numbers over 6,000 examples. Concerts and demonstrations are given regularly. Consultations are available by appointment.

Scotland

Dean Castle, Kilmarnock

Dean Castle houses one of Europe's finest collections of early musical instruments, especially lutes, guitars, spinets and small keyboard instruments, housed in the fifteenth-century palace, alongside a major collection of armour and tapestries. Consultations are available by appointment.

Edinburgh University Collection of Historical Musical Instruments

Among some 2,000 instruments of all types – plucked strings, woodwind, brass, percussion – is to be found the best collection of historical acoustic guitars in the country. The University also runs a sister collection, the Russell Collection of Early Keyboard Instruments, based at St Cecilia's Hall, Niddry Street, Cowgate, Edinburgh, Lothian EH1 1LJ, Wed–Sat: 2–5. Consultations are available by appointment.

Royal Museum of Scotland, Edinburgh

This is the museum for bagpipes: it has a large collection, European in scope, and a major research archive relating particularly to the history of the bagpipe in Scotland.

Rock and Pop Instruments

One of the things you might have noticed about the preceding museum list, is its almost complete absence of rock and roll instruments. Sadly, in the musical instrument collections of Britain, you are more likely to come across a palaeolithic bone whistle than an electric guitar. In most museums rock, if it appears at all, tends to be seen as a sociological rather than a musical phenomenon, and is represented in terms of its ephemera: designs for record sleeves and posters, Mick Jagger's jump suits, and the odd Sex Pistols' T-shirt. But the times they are a-changing. Auction houses now hold regular sales of pop memorabilia and instruments, and one of their major clients, the Hard Rock Café, has put together the world's largest collection of rock and roll effects.

✍ I. EXAMINATION, INVESTIGATION AND EXPERT WITNESSES

Examine the object as usual, recording all inscribed details, serial numbers, provenance, etc.

For information and valuations of rock and pop memorabilia, go to an auction house or dealer. For advice about the instruments themselves, your best bet is to contact a dealer in rock instruments – in London, Denmark Street has a good selection – or a reputable musicians' magazine (i.e. a publication that concentrates on instruments and equipment rather than pop stars and hairstyles) which should be able to refer you to a relevant expert. Currently acknowledged as the leader in this field is *Making Music* magazine, available from musical instrument shops and recording studios. *Making Music*, 20 Bowling Green Lane, London ECIR oBD. Tel: 071 251 1900.

📖 **BIBLIOGRAPHY**
Bacon, Tony and Day, Paul. *The Ultimate Guitar Book*, London, Dorling Kindersley, 1991
　Guru's Guitar Guide, London, Making Music, 1992
Duchessoir, A. R. *Guitar Identification*, Mediapresse, 1983
Gruhn, George. *A Guide to Vintage Guitars*, USA, 1991

22

The Media Pages:
Theatre, Photography, Film,
Television and Advertising

If your object or investigations relate in some form to the above subjects, then the following expert witnesses should be able to help. Obviously they are not the only institutions with collections in these various fields, but as specialist centres they are a good place to take your enquiries and to look for further clues. Refer to Part One for general information about conducting your investigation.

Theatre

✍ EXPERT WITNESSES AND MISCELLANEOUS SOURCES

Many museums have a small amount of theatrical material and some will include a section, or even a whole collection, devoted to a star who was born in the area. Costume and dress museums might be able to assist with enquiries about costume designs.

Certain major theatres could have preserved their own archival collections, for example, at Stratford and Covent

Garden, and local history libraries can be another valuable source of reference. For toy theatres see Pollock's Toy Museum.

🏛 SPECIALIST MUSEUMS

London

Theatre Museum

The museum specialises in theatre and all the live performing arts, including circus, music hall, ballet, opera, and puppetry. Objects in the collections are specific to performance rather than to the artist or craftsman who made them, and cover a broad range of media, including paintings, prints, ceramics, ephemera, costumes, books, and photographs. The library is open to the public by appointment, Tuesday to Friday. Consultations are available by appointment.

Regional

The Raymond Mander and Joe Mitchenson Theatre Collection, Beckenham

The collection includes a fine selection of theatrical memorabilia and ephemera, and is particularly strong in china and porcelain, including earthenware statuettes. There is a large photographic archive and material includes theatrical designs, letters, costumes and scripts. Telephone or write with any enquiries. Since the museum receives no public funding, a charge will be made for any research undertaken.

✉ ARCHIVE COLLECTIONS

The University of Bristol Theatre Collection
29 Park Row
Bristol BS1 5LT
Tel: 0272 303 218

The University has a major collection of published and archival material relating to the history of theatre and the performing arts in Britain. Their holdings include the London Old Vic Theatre Archives, the Beerbohm Tree Collection, and vast collections of programmes and stage designs.

Scottish Theatre Archives
Department of Special Collections
Glasgow University Library
Hillhead Street
Glasgow G12 8QE
Tel: 041 339 8855 x 6767

The University library holds published and archival material relating to theatre and the performing arts in Scotland.

Photography, Film and Television

✍ EXPERT WITNESSES AND MISCELLANEOUS SOURCES

Science museums house displays of cameras and photographic apparatus, and museums across the country include photography in their collections.

As well as the specialist centres listed below, more general institutions such as the V & A or the National Portrait Gallery might well be able to help you with enquiries about photographers. Across the country there will be small collections or indeed specific institutions, such as the Fox Talbot Museum of Photography in Lacock, Wilts., devoted to the work of local photographers and their associates. There are a number of commercial galleries concentrating on photography which could be of some assistance. For valuations and general advice, consult auction houses and specialist dealers (see Part One).

🏛 SPECIALIST MUSEUMS AND INSTITUTIONS

London

British Film Institute (BFI)
21 Stephen Street
London W1P 1PL
Tel: 071 255 1444

Founded to 'stimulate a wider public interest in the arts of film, video and television', the BFI offers a wide range of facilities to the detective, including the National Film Archive – the national repository of film and television in the UK – and BFI Library Services, the largest collection of documentation on film and television in the world. It also holds published and archival material, and ephemera. The library is open Mon–Fri: 10.30–5; Wed: 1.30–8. Day pass: £7 (£2 for BFI members).

Museum of the Moving Image

The museum illustrates the history of moving images from early Chinese shadow theatre to the latest film and television technology.

Photographers' Gallery
5 Great Newport Street
London WC2H 7HY
Tel: 071 831 1772

The gallery has a programme of changing exhibitions, and there is a strong emphasis on the work of living photographers. The reference library is open Tues, Thurs, Fri: 11–5, by appointment, it contains information on contemporary photography and other material.

Regional

National Museum of Photography, Film and Television, Bradford

As its title suggests, the museum explores the story, both past and present, of film, television and photography. The museum's library is open by appointment, and archives include records concerning Fox Talbot, Julia Margaret Cameron and the Kodak Collection. Consultations are held on the last Wednesday of the month. Phone for further details.

Royal Photographic Society National Centre of Photography, Bath

The collection includes major holdings of photographs and cameras, and the specialist library and archive are among the best in the world. Opinions and advice are available by appointment, and at least one week's notice must be given to use the library. The library is free to members and bona fide students, otherwise there is a small charge.

Advertising and Packaging

✍ EXPERT WITNESSES AND MISCELLANEOUS SOURCES

Museums and libraries throughout the country cover advertising and packaging in various forms, and individual firms and manufacturers could well have preserved material relating to their products and services.

🏛 SPECIALIST MUSEUMS AND ARCHIVES

Museum of Advertising and Packaging, Gloucester

The Museum of Advertising has displays of tins, bottles, papers, packets, posters, display cards, and consumer ephemera of all kinds. It is the largest collection of its type in the world, and the result of one man's personal passion for the disposable. Robert Opie, its creator, has written a number of books on packaging and related subjects, and is a major authority in this unusual field. Should you be researching the objects themselves, the development of graphic design or the history of advertising, this is an obvious place to visit.

National Bottle Museum, Elsecar

This is a new museum devoted to the history of bottles, packaging and containers. Its co-ordinator, Alan Blakeman, is also the editor of the *British Bottle Review*, the UK-based national and international magazine for antique bottle collectors, and the perfect source for enquiries about bottles, pot lids, etc. For further information contact:

BBR Publishing
2 Stratford Avenue
Elsecar
Barnsley
South Yorkshire S74 8AA

The Advertising Archives
150 Southampton Row
London WC1B 5AL
Tel: 071 837 4426

The archives hold the largest collection of press advertising and illustration in Europe from the 1870s to the present day, and published and printed material related to advertising both historical and contemporary. It is a good place for research, advice and valuations on advertising illustrations and ephemera.

Sects and Societies

If the object you are investigating has any connection with a specific sect, society or recognised group of people, you should try to find out if they have a museum or archive which could possibly help you with your enquiries. For example, should you be researching a piece of masonic glass or porcelain, it might be worth contacting the freemasons' museum.

Grand Lodge Library and Museum

The museum is concerned with freemasonry throughout the world, from the eighteenth century to the present day. In addition to regalia, there are large collections of silver, glass, pottery, porcelain, and anything that has had a masonic use or bears masonic decoration. The library is open by request, and identifications and advice are given by appointment.

Similarly, if your piece relates to the Order of St John, try their collection.

Museum and Library of the Order of St John

The museum specialises in material relating to the history of the Order of St John and to the St John Ambulance Association and Brigade. The collection includes silver, medals, furniture, textiles, armour, paintings, prints and drawings. Items can be brought in by appointment. The library is open to the public by prior arrangement.

The Jewish Museum might be able to help with enquiries about Judaica; The Huguenot Society (Huguenot Library, University College, Gower Street, London WC1, Tel: 071 380 7094) with investigations into Huguenot craftsmen; and the Jesuit archive (Jesuit Church, Farm Street, London W1, Tel: 071 493 7811) with research relating to the portrait of a Jesuit ancestor.

For a list of similar small and specific museums, consult a good museum guide. Other useful sources for addresses include directories of associations, and telephone directories, particularly those for London.

Whatever the subject of your investigations, use your imagination to track down clues, and try any available source of information. Expert witnesses, however esoteric your field, are often only a phone call away.

Foreign Sources and Americana

Depending on what you are researching you might well find that you need to consult foreign reference books and to get in touch with museums outside Britain. At some stage you might require some translation services. Obviously many of the museums and libraries included in this book will have extensive knowledge and/or collections of foreign material, and will be able to put you in touch with the right sources. In addition to these, a number of foreign countries have cultural institutes in Britain, where you will find library facilities, translators and other possibly useful contacts. Many of these are situated in London, and will be in the telephone book, but if you cannot find them there, consult the relevant embassy for details.

In one particular instance, you do not even have to leave the country to consult a foreign museum:

The American Museum in Britain

The museum specialises in the American decorative arts (seventeenth to nineteenth centuries), American folk art, textiles, rugs, and other material. The library, concentrating on American art, architecture and history, can be consulted by appointment. Though many museums cover American subjects in their own fields, this could certainly be a useful source of specialist advice.

Appendix: Museum Directory

Museum of Advertising and
  Packaging
The Albert Warehouse
Gloucester Docks
Gloucester GL1 2EH
Tel: 0452 302309
Tues–Sun: 10–6 (10–5 in winter)

Allhallows Museum
High Street
Honiton
Devon EX14 8PE
Tel: 0404 44966
May–Sept, Mon–Sat: 10–5; Oct,
  Mon–Sat: 10–4

The American Museum in
  Britain
Claverton Manor
Bath BA2 7BD
Tel: 0225 460503
Museum, Tues–Sun: 2–5
Office and Library, Mon–Fri:
  9.30–12.30, 2.30–5.30
Library open by appointment

Ashmolean Museum of Art and
  Archaeology
Beaumont Street
Oxford OX1 2PH
Tel: 0865 278000
Tues–Sat: 10–4; Sun: 2–4
Print Room, Mon: 10–1, 2–4

Bantock House Museum
Bantock Park
Wolverhampton
West Midlands WV3 9LQ
Tel: 0902 312132
Mon–Fri: 10–7; Sat: 10–5; Sun:
  2–5

The Bate Collection of Historic
  Instruments
University of Oxford Faculty of
  Music
St Aldate's
Oxford OX1 1DB
Tel: 0865 276139
Mon–Fri: 2–4 (term time)

Bethnal Green Museum of
  Childhood
Cambridge Heath Road
Bethnal Green
London E2 9PA
Tel: 081 980 3204
Mon–Thurs, Sat: 10–6; Sun:
  2.30–6
Library open by appointment

Birmingham City Museum and
  Art Gallery
Chamberlain Square
Birmingham B3 3DH
Tel: 021 235 2834
Mon–Sat: 9.30–5; Sun: 2–5

Boosey and Hawkes Museum
Deansbrook Road
Edgware
Middlesex HA8 9RB
Tel: 081 952 7711
Wed, by appointment

The Bowes Museum
Barnard Castle
Co Durham DL12 8NP
Tel: 0833 690606
Museum, Mon–Sat: 10–5; Sun:
  2–5 (Nov–Feb: until 4)
Library, Thurs: 2–5; Sat: 10–12

Brighton Museum and Art
  Gallery
Church Street
Brighton BN1 1UE
Tel: 0273 603005
Tues–Sat: 10–5.45; Sun: 2–5
Opinions, Wed: 2.30–4, by
  appointment

City of Bristol Museum and Art
  Gallery
Queen's Road
Bristol
Avon BS8 1RL
Tel: 0272 299771
Mon–Sat: 10–5

The British Museum
Great Russell Street
London WC1B 3DG
Tel: 071 636 1555
Mon–Sat: 10–5; Sun: 2.30–6
Opinion times vary among
  departments, so telephone for
  details

Broadfield House Glass Museum
Compton Drive
Kingswinford
West Midlands DY6 9QA
Tel: 0384 273011
Tues–Fri: 2–5; Sat: 10–1, 2–5;
  Sun: 2–5

The Burrell Collection
Pollock Country Park
2060 Pollockshaws Road
Glasgow G43 1AT
Tel: 041 649 7151
Mon–Sat: 10–5; Sun: 11–5

Cambridge University Museum
  of Archaeology and
  Anthropology
Downing Street
Cambridge CB2 3DZ
Tel: 0223 337722
Mon–Fri: 2–4; Sat: 10–12.30

The Centre for the Study of
Cartoon and Caricature
The Library
University of Kent
Canterbury CT2 7NU
Tel: 0227 764000 ext 3127

Cheltenham Art Gallery and
Museum
Clarence Street
Cheltenham
Gloucestershire GL50 3JT
Tel: 0242 237431
Mon–Sat: 10–5.20; 1 May–
30 Sept, Sun: 2–5.20
Opinions, Wed: 2–5, by
appointment

Chester Beatty Library and
Gallery of Oriental Art
20 Shrewsbury Road
Dublin 4
Ireland
Tel: 010 353 12 692 386
Tues–Fri: 10–1, 2.30–5.15;
Sat: 2–5
Library open by appointment,
but see page 186

The Chester Toy and Doll
Museum
13A Lower Bridge Street
Chester CH1 1RS
Tel: 0244 346297
Mon–Sat: 11–5
Opinions, Sat morning

The Clock Museum
Angel Corner
8 Angel Hill
Bury St Edmunds
Suffolk IP33 1UZ
Tel: 0284 757072

Mon–Sat: 10–5; Sun: 2–5
Opinions, Wed afternoon
Library open by appointment

Clydebank District Museum
Old Town Hall
Dunbarton Road
Clydebank G81 1XQ
Tel: 041 941 1331
Mon, Wed: 2–4.30; Sat: 10–4.30

Concertina Museum Collection
Rear Flat
Old Chapel
Belper
Derby SE5 1NZ
Tel: 0773 827910/820566

Museum of Costume
Assembly Rooms
Bennett Street
Bath BA1 2QH
Tel: 0225 461111
Telephone for opening times
Opinions, Thurs and Fri
afternoons by appointment
See also Fashion Research Centre,
Bath

Museum of Costume and
Textiles
51 Castle Gate
Nottingham NG1 6AF
Tel: 0602 483504
Mon–Sun: 10–5
Library open by appointment

Darlington Art Gallery
Crown Street
Darlington DL1 1ND
Tel: 0325 462034
Mon–Fri: 10–8; Sat: 10–5.30

Dean Castle and Museum
Dean Road
Kilmarnock KA1 3BU
Tel: 0563 26401
Mon–Sun: 12–5

City of Derby Museums and Art
    Gallery
The Strand
Derby DE1 1BS
Tel: 0332 255586
Mon: 11–5; Tues–Sat: 10–5; Sun
    and Bank Holidays: 2–5

The Design Museum
28 Shad Thames
Butlers Wharf
London SE1 2YD
Tel: 071 403 6933
Tues–Sun: 11.30–6.30
Library, Tues–Sat: 11.30–6.30

Devonshire Collection of Period
    Costume
Bogan House
43 High Street
Totnes
Devon TQ9 5RY
Tel: 0803 862857
Spring Bank Holiday–1 Oct,
    Mon–Fri: 11–5; Sun: 2–5
Library open by appointment

Doncaster Museum and Art
    Gallery
Chequer Road
Doncaster
South Yorkshire DN1 2AE
Tel: 0302 734 287
Mon–Sat: 10–5; Sun: 2–5

Sir Henry Doulton Gallery
Royal Doulton Ltd
Nile Street
Burslem
Stoke-on-Trent
Staffordshire ST6 2AJ
Tel: 0782 575 454
Mon–Fri: 9–4.30

Dyson Perrin Museum Trust
Severn Street
Worcester WR1 2NE
Tel: 0905 23221
Mon–Fri: 9.30–5; Sat: 10–5

Edinburgh University Collection
    of Historic Musical
    Instruments
Reid Concert Hall
Bristo Square
Edinburgh
Lothian EH8 9AG
Tel: 031 650 1000
Wed, Sat: 2–5

The Fan Museum
10–12 Crooms Hill
Greenwich
London SE10 8ER
Tel: 081 858 7879/305 1441
Telephone for opening times

Fashion Research Centre
4 Circus
Bath BA1 2EW
Tel: 0225 461111 ext 2752
Mon–Sat: 9.30–5
Opinions, Thurs, Fri: 2.15–3.15,
    by appointment

Ferens Art Gallery
Queen Victoria Square
Hull HU1 3RA
Tel: 0482 222750
Mon–Sat: 10–5; Sun: 1.30–4.30

Also:
Town Docks Museum
Queen Victoria Square
Hull HU1 3DX
Tel: 0482 222737
Mon–Sat: 10–5; Sun: 1.30–4.30

Fitzwilliam Museum
Trumpington Street
Cambridge CB2 1RB
Tel: 0223 337733/332900
Tues–Sat: 10–5; Sun: 2.15–5

The Gallery of English Costume
Platt Hall
Platt Fields
Rusholme
Manchester M14 5LL
Tel: 061 224 5217
Mon, Wed–Sat: 10–6; Sun: 2–6
   (Nov–Feb: until 4)
Library open by appointment

Geffrye Museum
Kingsland Road
London E2 8EA
Tel: 071 739 9893
Tues–Sat: 10–5; Sun: 2–5

The Geological Museum
Exhibition Road
London SW7 2DE
Tel: 071 589 3444
Mon–Sat: 10–6; Sun: 2.30–6

Glasgow Art Gallery and
   Museum
Kelvingrove
Glasgow G3 8AG
Tel: 041 357 3929
Mon–Sat: 10–5; Sun: 2–5

Glynn Vivian Art Gallery and
   Museum
Alexandra Road
Swansea SA1 5DZ
Tel: 0792 655006
Mon–Sun: 10.30–5.30
Library open by appointment

Grand Lodge Library and
   Museum
Freemasons' Hall
Great Queen Street
London WC2B 5AZ
Tel: 071 831 9811 ext 260
Mon–Fri: 10–5;
   Sat: by appointment
Library open by appointment

Graves Art Gallery
Surrey Street
Sheffield S1 1XZ
Tel: 0742 734781
Mon–Sat: 10–6
Opinions, Wed: 12–2

Grosvenor Museum
27 Grosvenor Street
Chester CH1 2DD
Tel: 0244 321616
Mon–Sat: 10.30–5; Sun: 2–5

Guildhall Library and Print
  Room
Aldermanbury
London EC2P 2EJ
Art Gallery, Tel: 071 606 3030;
  Mon–Sat: 10–5
Library, Tel: 071 260 1868/1870;
  Mon–Sat: 9.30–5
Manuscripts, Tel: 071 260 1863;
  Mon–Sat: 9.30–4.45
Prints, Maps and Drawings, Tel:
  071 260 1839; Mon–Fri: 9.30–5

Herbert Art Gallery and Museum
Jordan Well
Coventry CV1 5RW
Tel: 0203 832381/86
Mon–Sat: 10–5.30; Sun: 2–5
Library open by appointment

Museum of the History of
  Science
The Old Ashmolean Building
Broad Street
Oxford OX1 3AZ
Tel: 0865 43997
Mon–Fri: 10.30–1, 2.30–4

Horniman Museum
London Road
Forest Hill
London SE23 3PQ
Tel: 081 699 2339
Mon–Sat: 10.30–5.50; Sun:
  2–5.50
Library, Tues–Sat: 10.30–5.45;
  Sun: 2–5.45

Hove Museum and Art Gallery
19 New Church Road
Hove
East Sussex BN3 4AB
Tel: 0273 779410
Tues–Fri: 10–5; Sat: 10–4.30;
  Sun: 2–5

The Hugh Lane Municipal
  Gallery of Modern Art
Charlemont House
Parnell Square
Dublin 1
Ireland
Tel: 010 353 1 741 903
Tues–Sat: 9.30–6; Sun: 11–5

Hunterian Art Gallery
University of Glasgow
82 Hillhead Street
Glasgow G12 8QQ
Tel: 041 330 5431
Mon–Fri: 9.30–5; Sat: 9.30–1
Library open by appointment

Hunterian Museum
University of Glasgow
University Avenue
Glasgow G12 8QQ
Tel: 041 330 4221
Mon–Fri: 9.30–5; Sat: 9.30–1

Imperial War Museum
Lambeth Road
London SE1 6HZ
Tel: 071 735 8922
Mon–Sun: 10–6
Library open by appointment

Ironbridge Gorge Museum Trust
The Wharfage
Ironbridge
Telford TF8 7AW
Tel: 095245 3522 (offices),
  2751 (library)
Mar–Oct, Mon–Sun: 10–6; Nov–
  Feb, Mon–Sun: 10–5

Jewish Museum
Woburn House
Upper Woburn Place
London WC1H 0EP
Tel: 071 388 4525
Tues–Thurs: 10–4; Fri, Sun: 10–
  12.45 (summer, Fri: until 4)

Judges' Lodgings
Church Street
Lancaster
Lancashire LA1 1YS
Tel: 0524 32808
Opening times vary throughout
  the year, so telephone before
  visiting

Kidderminster Museum and Art
  Gallery
Market Street
Kidderminster
Worcestershire DY10 1AB
Tel: 0562 66610
Telephone for opening times

Laing Art Gallery
Higham Place
Newcastle-upon-Tyne NE1 8AG
Tel: 091 232 7734/232 6989
Tues–Fri: 10–5.30; Sat: 10–4.30;
  Sun: 2.30–5.30

Lancaster City Museum
Market Square
Lancaster
Lancashire LA1 1HT
Tel: 0524 64637
Mon–Sat: 10–5
Library open by appointment

Leeds City Art Gallery
The Headrow
Leeds LS1 3AA
Tel: 0531 462495
Mon, Tues, Thurs, Fri: 10–6;
  Wed: 10–9; Sat: 10–4;
  Sun: 2–5

Liverpool Museum
William Brown Street
Liverpool L3 8EN
Tel: 051 207 0001
Mon–Sat: 10–5; Sun: 12.30–5

London Toy and Model Museum
21 Craven Hill
London W2 3EN
Tel: 071 262 7905/9450
Tues–Sat: 10–5.30; Sun: 11–5.30

Manchester City Art Gallery
Mosley Street
Manchester M2 3JL
Tel: 061 236 9422
Mon–Sat: 10–6; Sun: 2–6
Opinions, Wed: 2–4

The Manchester Museum
The University of Manchester
Oxford Road
Manchester M13 9PL
Tel: 061 273 3333 ext 3101
Mon–Sat: 10–5

Museum of Mankind
British Museum Department of
    Ethnography
6 Burlington Gardens
London W1X 2EX
Tel: 071 437 2224
Mon–Sat: 10–5; Sun: 2.30–6
Students' Room, Mon–Sat:
    1–4.45

The Minton Museum
Minton House
London Road
Stoke-on-Trent
Staffordshire ST4 7QD
Tel: 0782 744 766
Mon–Fri: 9–12.30, 1.15–4.30

Museum of the Moving Image
South Bank
Waterloo
London SE1 8XT
Tel: 071 928 3535
Tues–Sat: 10–8; Sun: 10–6

The Musical Museum
368 High Street
Brentford
Middlesex TW8 0BD
Tel: 081 560 8108
Apr–Oct, Sat, Sun: 2–5; guided
    tour: Tues and Fri afternoons

National Army Museum
Royal Hospital Road
Chelsea
London SW3 4HT
Tel: 071 730 0717
Mon–Sat: 10–5.30; Sun: 2–5.30
Reading Room, Tues–Sat:
    10–4.30

National Bottle Museum
Elsecar Project
Wath Road
Elsecar
Nr Barnsley
South Yorkshire S74 8HJ
Tel: 0226 745 156
Telephone for opening times

National Gallery
Trafalgar Square
London WC2N 5DN
Tel: 071 839 3321
Mon–Sat: 10–6; Sun: 2–6
Opinions, Wed: 2.30–5

The National Gallery of Ireland
Merrion Square West
Dublin 2
Ireland
Tel: 010 353 1 608 533
Mon–Sat: 10–6; Sun: 2–5

National Gallery of Scotland
The Mound
Edinburgh EH2 2EL
Tel: 031 556 8921
Mon–Sat: 10–5; Sun: 2–5

National Maritime Museum
Romney Road
Greenwich
London SE10 9NF
Tel: 081 858 4422
Mon–Sat: 10–6; Sun: 2–6
Library, Mon–Fri: 10–4.45;
    Sat: by appointment

National Museum of Ireland
Kildare Street
Dublin 2
Ireland
Tel: 010 353 1 618811
Tues–Sat: 10–5; Sun: 2–5

National Museum of
   Photography, Film and
   Television
Prince's View
Bradford
West Yorkshire BD5 0TR
Tel: 0274 727488
Tues–Sun: 10.30–6
Opinions, last Wed of every
   month

National Museum of Science and
   Industry
Exhibition Road
London SW7 2DD
Tel: 071 938 8181
Library, Tel: 071 938 8284
Mon–Sat: 10–6; Sun: 11–6

National Museum of Wales
Cathays Park
Cardiff
South Glamorgan CF1 3NP
Tel: 0222 397951
Tues–Sat: 10–5; Sun: 2.30–5

National Portrait Gallery (NPG)
St Martin's Place
London WC2H 0HE
Tel: 071 930 1552
Mon–Fri: 10–5; Sat: 10–6;
   Sun: 2–6

Also:
NPG Archive and Library
The Mill
72 Molesworth Street
Lewisham SE13 7EY
Tel: 071 318 2888
Mon–Fri: 10–1, 2–5, by
   appointment only

National Railway Museum
Leeman Road
York YO2 4XJ
Tel: 0904 621261
Mon–Sat: 10–6; Sun: 2.30–6
Reading Room, Mon–Fri:
   10.30–5, by appointment

Natural History Museum
Department of Library Services
Cromwell Road
London SW7 5BD
Tel: 071 938 8971
Mon–Fri: 10–4.30

Newarke Houses Museum
The Newarke
Leicester LE2 7BY
Tel: 0533 554100 ext 3222
Mon–Sat: 10–5.30; Sun: 2–5.30
Library open by appointment

Northampton Central Museum
   and Art Gallery
Guildhall Road
Northampton NN1 1DP
Tel: 0604 34881 ext 394
Mon–Sat: 10–5; Thurs: 10–8

Northampton Museum of
   Leathercraft
60 Bridge Street
Northampton NN1 1DP
Tel: 0604 34881
Mon–Sat: 10–5
Library open by appointment

Norwich Castle Museum
Norwich NR1 3JU
Tel: 0603 222222 ext 71235
Mon–Sat: 10–5; Sun: 2–5
Opinions, Wed

Museum and Library of the
   Order of St John
St John's Gate
St John's Lane
Clerkenwell
London EC1M 4DA
Tel: 071 253 6644
Mon–Fri: 10–5; Sat: 10–4
Library open by appointment

Oriental Museum
Durham University
Elvet Hall
Durham DH1 3TH
Tel: 091 374 2911
Mon–Sat: 9.30–1, 2–5; Sun: 2–5
   (Nov–Feb: closed weekends)

Percival David Foundation of
   Chinese Art
53 Gordon Square
London WC1H 0PD
Tel: 071 387 3909
Mon–Fri: 10–5
Library, Mon–Fri: 10.30–1,
   2–4.45, by appointment

Pilkington Glass Museum
Prescot Road
St Helens
Lancashire WA10 3TT
Tel: 0744 28882 ext 2499/2014/
   2727
Telephone for opening times
Library open by appointment

Pitshanger Manor Museum
Manor Lane
London W5 5EQ
Tel: 081 567 1227 or 081 579 2424
   ext 42683
Tues–Sat: 10–5

Pitt-Rivers Museum
South Parks Road
Oxford OX1 3PP
Tel: 0865 270927
Mon–Sat: 1–4.30
Telephone for library opening
   times

Pollock's Toy Museum
1 Scala Street
London W1P 1LT
Tel: 071 636 3452
Mon–Sat: 10–5

Prescot Museum of Clock and
   Watchmaking
34 Church Street
Prescot
Merseyside L34 3LA
Tel: 051 430 7787
Tues–Sat: 10–5; Sun: 2–5

The Raymond Mander and Joe
   Mitchenson Theatre Collection
The Mansion
Beckenham Place Park
Beckenham
Kent BR3 2BP
Tel: 081 658 7725
Mon–Fri: 10–5

Ribchester Museum of
   Childhood
Church Street
Ribchester
Lancashire PR3 3YE
Tel: 0254 878 520
Tues–Sun: 10.30–5
Library open by appointment

Rotherham Art Gallery
Walker Place
Rotherham
South Yorkshire S65 1JH
Tel: 0709 382121
Mon, Wed–Fri: 10–6; Sat: 10–5

Also:
Clifton Park Museum
Clifton Lane
Rotherham
South Yorkshire S65 2AA
Tel: 0709 382121
Mon–Thurs: 10–5; Sat: 10–5;
   Sun: 2–5

Rougemont House Museum of
   Costume and Lace
Castle Street
Exeter EX4 3RX
Tel: 0392 265360
Mon–Sat: 10–5.30
Opinions, Thurs: 2–5, by
   appointment

Royal Academy of Arts Library
Burlington House
Piccadilly
London W1V 0DS
Tel: 071 439 7438
Mon–Fri: 10–1, 2–5, by
   appointment

Royal Air Force Museum
Grahame Park Way
Hendon
London NW9 5LL
Tel: 081 205 2266
Mon–Sun: 10–6

Royal Albert Memorial Museum
Queen Street
Exeter EX4 3RX
Tel: 0392 265858
Tues–Sat: 10–5.30

The Royal Armouries
HM Tower of London
London EC3N 4AB
Tel: 071 480 6358
Museum, Mon–Sat: 9.30–5; Nov–
   Feb, Mon–Sat: 9.30–4; Sun: 2–5
Library, Mon–Fri: 10–12, 2–5

Royal Brierly Crystal
North Street
Brierly Hill
West Midlands DY5 3SJ
Tel: 0384 70161
Telephone for opening times

Royal College of Music
Prince Consort Road
London SW7 2BS
Tel: 071 589 3643
Musical Instrument Museum,
   Wed: 2–4.30 (term time)
Library, Mon–Fri: 10.30–5

Royal Crown Derby Museum
Royal Crown Derby Porcelain
   Co Ltd
194 Osmaston Road
Derby DE3 8JZ
Tel: 0332 47051
Mon–Fri: 10–4

Royal Institute of British
  Architects
Drawings Collection
21 Portman Square
London W1H 9HF
Tel: 071 580 5533
Mon–Fri: 9.30–5.30, by
  appointment

Royal Museum of Scotland
The Royal Museum occupies two
sites: Chambers Street is devoted
to archaeology, natural history,
geology, European decorative
arts, and sculpture – in brief, it is
a major international collection;
Queen Street concentrates on
Scottish art and culture in all its
manifestations from prehistoric
times onwards. All enquiries
should be addressed to:
Chambers Street
Edinburgh EH1 1JF
Tel: 031 225 7534
Mon–Sat: 10–5; Sun: 2–5
Library open by appointment

Royal Photographic Society
  National Centre of
  Photography
The Octagon
Milsom Street
Bath BA1 1DN
Tel: 0225 462841
Mon–Sat: 9.30–5.30
Library open by appointment

Royal Scottish Academy
The Mound
Edinburgh EH2 2EL
Tel: 031 225 6671
Library, Mon–Fri: 10–1, 2–4.30,
  by appointment

Royal Society of Painters-
  Printmakers
Royal Watercolour Society
Bankside Gallery
48 Hopton Street
London SE1 9JH
Tel: 071 928 7521
Telephone for opening times
Library open by appointment

St John's House
St John's
Warwick CV34 4NE
Tel: 0926 412132
Costume Study Room, Tel: 0926
  412021
Mon–Sat: 10–12.30, 1.30–5.30;
  May–Sept, Sun: 2.30–5.30

Science Museum, *see* National
  Museum of Science and
  Industry

Scottish National Gallery of
  Modern Art
Bedford Road
Edinburgh EH4 3DR
Tel: 031 556 8921
Mon–Sat: 10–5; Sun: 2–5
Library open by appointment

Scottish National Portrait Gallery
1 Queen Street
Edinburgh EH2 1JD
Tel: 031 556 8921
Mon–Sat: 10–5; Sun: 2–5
Opinions, Thurs
Library open by appointment

Scottish Tartans Society and
    Museum
Davidson House
Drummond Street
Comrie
Perthshire PH6 2DW
Tel: 0764 79779
Telephone for opening times

Sheffield City Museum
Weston Park
Norton Lees Lane
Sheffield S10 2TP
Tel: 0742 368588
Tues–Sat: 10–5; Sun: 11–5
Library open by appointment

The Shoe Museum
C. & J. Clark Ltd
40 High Street
Street
Somerset BA16 0YA
Tel: 0458 43131 ext 2169
Easter Mon–31 Oct, Mon–Fri:
    10–4.45; Sat: 10–4.30

Silver Studio Collection
Middlesex Polytechnic
Bounds Green Road
London N11 2NQ
Tel: 081 368 1299 ext 7339
Mon–Fri: 10–4, by appointment
    only
Library open by appointment

Sir John Soane's Museum
13 Lincoln's Inn Fields
London WC2A 3BP
Tel: 071 405 2107
Museum, Tues–Sat: 10–5
Library, Tues–Fri: 10–1, 2–5;
    Sat: 10–1, by appointment

Spode Museum
Church Street
Stoke-on-Trent
Staffordshire ST4 1BX
Tel: 0782 744011
Mon–Thurs: 10–4.30; Fri: 10–
    12.30; visits by appointment

The Stained Glass Museum
The North Triforium
Ely Cathedral
Ely
Cambridgeshire
Tel: 0223 327367
Mar–Oct, Mon–Fri: 10.30–4; Sat
    and Bank Holidays: 10.30–4.30;
    Sun: 12–3

Stoke-on-Trent City Museum
    and Art Gallery
Bethesda Street
Hanley
Stoke-on-Trent
Staffordshire ST1 3DE
Tel: 0782 202173
Mon–Sat: 10–5; Sun: 2–5
Opinions, Wed: 2–4.30

Sunderland Pottery
Sunderland Museum and Art
    Gallery
Borough Road
Sunderland SR1 1PP
Tel: 091 514 1235 ext 153
Tues–Fri: 10–5.30; Sat: 10–4; Sun:
    2–5; closed Mon except Bank
    Holidays

Tate Gallery
Millbank
London SW1P 4RG
Tel: 071 821 1313
Mon–Sat: 10–5.50; Sun: 2–5.50
Library open by appointment

Temple Newsam House
Leeds
West Yorkshire LS15 0AE
Tel: 0532 647321
Tues–Sun: 10.30–6.15 (dusk in
   winter)
Library open by appointment

Theatre Museum
1E Tavistock Street
London WC2E 7PA
Tel: 071 836 7891
Tues–Sun: 11–7
Library, Tues–Fri: by
   appointment

Tunbridge Wells Museum and
   Art Gallery
Civic Centre
Mount Pleasant
Royal Tunbridge Wells
Kent TN1 1NS
Tel: 0892 26121
Mon–Sat: 10–5
Library open by appointment

Ulster Museum
Botanic Gardens
Belfast BT9 5AB
Tel: 0232 381251
Mon–Fri: 10–5; Sat: 1–5;
   Sun: 2–5

Usher Gallery
Lindum Road
Lincoln LE11 1AR
Tel: 0522 27980
Mon–Sat: 10–5.30; Sun: 2.30–5
Opinions, Tues afternoon and Fri
   morning

The Victoria & Albert Museum
Cromwell Road
London SW7 2RL
Tel: 071 938 8500
Mon–Sat: 10–5.50;
   Sun: 2.30–5.50
Print Room: Tues–Fri: 10–4.30;
   Sat: 10–1, 2–4.30
Opinions (all depts), Tues: 2.30–
   4.30
See also National Art Library,
   page 28

The Museum of Victorian Reed
   Organs
Victoria Hall
Victoria Road
Saltaire
Shipley
West Yorkshire BD18 4PS
Tel: 0274 585601
Mon–Sun: 11–4

Walker Art Gallery
William Brown Street
Liverpool L3 8EL
Tel: 051 207 0001
Mon–Sat: 10–5; Sun: 2–5
Opinions, Thurs: 2–4
Library open by appointment

The Wallace Collection
Hertford House
Manchester Square
London W1M 6BN
Tel: 071 935 0687
Mon–Sat: 10–5; Sun: 2–5

Warwick Doll Museum
Oken's House
Castle Street
Warwick CV34
Tel: 0926 494456
Telephone for opening times

Wedgwood Museum
Barlaston
Stoke-on-Trent
Staffordshire ST12 9ES
Tel: 0782 204141
Easter–Oct, Mon–Fri: 9–5;
  Sat: 10–4
Library open by appointment

The West Highland Museum
Cameron Square
Fort William
Inverness-shire PH33 6AJ
Tel: 0397 2169
Oct–May, Mon–Sat: 10–1, 2–5;
  June and Sept, Mon–Sat: 9.30–
  5.30; July–Aug, Mon–Sat:
  9.30–9
Library open by appointment

Whipple Museum of the History
  of Science
Free School Lane
Cambridge CB2 3RH
Tel: 0223 334540
Mon–Fri: 2–4
Library open by appointment

Whitworth Art Gallery
University of Manchester
Oxford Road
Manchester M15 6ER
Tel: 061 273 4865
Mon, Wed, Fri, Sat: 10–5;
Thurs: 10–9
Opinions, last Thurs of every
  month, by appointment
Library open by appointment

William Morris Gallery
Water House
Lloyd Park
Forest Road
Walthamstow
London E17 4PP
Tel: 081 527 5544 ext 4390
Tues–Sat: 10–1, 2–5; first Sun of
  every month: 10–12, 2–5

Williamson Art Gallery and
  Museum
Slatey Road
Birkenhead
Merseyside L43 4UE
Tel: 051 652 4177
Mon–Sat: 10–5; Sun: 2–5

Wolverhampton Art Gallery and
  Museum
Lichfield Street
Wolverhampton WV1 1DU
Mon–Sat: 10–6
Library open by appointment

Wycombe Local History and
  Chair Museum
Castle Hill House
Priory Avenue
High Wycombe
Buckinghamshire HP13 6PX
Tel: 0494 23879
Mon–Sat: 10–1, 2–5

Yorkshire Museum
Museum Gardens
York YO1 2DR
Tel: 0904 629745
Mon–Sat: 10–5; Sun: 1–5
Library open by appointment

Index

The Art Detective's Notebook